M

Mathematical Models for Supply Ch

Mohamed Elhassan Seliaman

Mathematical Models for Supply Chain Inventory Coordination

Industrial Computing and Modeling

LAP LAMBERT Academic Publishing

Impressum / Imprint

Bibliografische Information der Deutschen Nationalbibliothek: Die Deutsche Nationalbibliothek verzeichnet diese Publikation in der Deutschen Nationalbibliografie; detaillierte bibliografische Daten sind im Internet über http://dnb.d-nb.de abrufbar. Alle in diesem Buch genannten Marken und Produktnamen unterliegen warenzeichen-, marken- oder patentrechtlichem Schutz bzw. sind Warenzeichen oder eingetragene Warenzeichen der jeweiligen Inhaber. Die Wiedergabe von Marken, Produktnamen, Gebrauchsnamen, Handelsnamen, Warenbezeichnungen u.s.w. in diesem Werk berechtigt auch ohne besondere Kennzeichnung nicht zu der Annahme, dass solche Namen im Sinne der Warenzeichen- und Markenschutzgesetzgebung als frei zu betrachten wären und daher von jedermann benutzt werden dürften.

Bibliographic information published by the Deutsche Nationalbibliothek: The Deutsche Nationalbibliothek lists this publication in the Deutsche Nationalbibliografie; detailed bibliographic data are available in the Internet at http://dnb.d-nb.de. Any brand names and product names mentioned in this book are subject to trademark, brand or patent protection and are trademarks or registered trademarks of their respective holders. The use of brand names, product names, common names, trade names, product descriptions etc. even without a particular marking in this works is in no way to be construed to mean that such names may be regarded as unrestricted in respect of trademark and brand protection legislation and could thus be used by anyone.

Coverbild / Cover image: www.ingimage.com

Verlag / Publisher:
LAP LAMBERT Academic Publishing
ist ein Imprint der / is a trademark of
OmniScriptum GmbH & Co. KG
Heinrich-Böcking-Str. 6-8, 66121 Saarbrücken, Deutschland / Germany
Email: info@lap-publishing.com

Herstellung: siehe letzte Seite /
Printed at: see last page
ISBN: 978-3-8484-1048-4

Zugl. / Approved by: Johor Bahro, Universiti Tekonologi Malaysia, Diss.2010

Mathematical Models for Supply Chain Inventory Coordination

Mohamed Elhassan Seliaman

Acknowledgements

All praise is to the Almighty Allah for his limitless help and guidance. Peace and blessings of Allah be upon his prophet Mohamed.

I would like to express my appreciation to Dr. Ab Rahman bin Ahmad and Dr. Mohamad Ishak Desa from Universiti Teknologi Malaysia (UTM) for their valuable comments and feedback on this work.

I am also indebted to my dearest family, especially my mother, my father, my wife, and my children Elaf, Ammar, Ahmad and Omar, for their constant love, purity of soul and inspiration to complete this book.

Preface

Numerous books and articles in supply chain modeling have been written in response to the global competition. However, most of the developed supply chain inventory models deal with two-stage supply chains. Even when multi-stage supply chains are considered, most of the developed models are based on restrictive assumptions such as of the deterministic demand. But Supply chains are stochastic in nature. Therefore, there is a need to analyze models that relax the usual assumptions to allow for a more realistic analysis of the supply chain inventory coordination. The main topic of this book is modeling supply chain inventory coordination under different situations. It presents several new useful models that can be easily applied to achieve key goals of supply chain management.

Contents

Chapter 1

Introduction to Supply chain Management and Inventory Coordination

1.1 Supply Chain Management

In the past, supply chain production-inventory decisions were not coordinated among the different parties in the supply chain. This lack of coordination lead to weakly connected processes and isolated decisions across the supply chain. Recently firms realized the need to improve their system performance and cost efficiency through closer collaboration among the chain partners and through high level of coordination of various decisions. The significant advances in information and communication technologies and the growing focus on supply chain management (SCM) have also motivated this tendency towards full integration and close collaboration.

The term Supply chain management seems to have emerged in the late 1980s and since then many definitions of SCM have been proposed (Nahmias, 2001). In this introduction, we will present few of them. According to Stanford Supply chain forum, Supply chain management deals with the management of materials, information and financial flows in a network consisting of suppliers, manufacturers, distributors, and customers. The goal of supply chain management is to enhance the competitive performance of the entire supply chain via efficient integration of the different chain members. This efficient integration requires that the flow of products and information among the supply chain members is managed in cooperative manner

1

that can achieve the goals of minimizing the system-wide costs and meeting service level requirements (Simchi-Levi et al.,2003).

Ross (1998) defines supply chain management as a continuously evolving management philosophy that seeks to unify the collective productive competencies and resources of the business functions found both within the enterprise and outside the firm's allied business partners located along intersecting supply channels into a highly competitive, customer-enriching supply system focused on developing innovative solution and synchronizing the flow of marketplace products, services, and information to create unique individualized sources of customers, Nahmias (2001). Ellram (1991) defines Supply chain management as a coordinated approach for managing the flow of goods from suppliers to ultimate consumers.

Supply chain management is mainly aimed at enhancing the competitive performance of the entire supply chain via efficient integration of the different chain members. This integration includes functional integration, spatial integration, and intertemporal integration. Functional integration refers to integration of purchasing, manufacturing, transportation, warehousing and inventory management activities. Spatial integration refers to integration of these activities across geographically dispersed vendors, facilities and markets. Intertemporal integration refers to the integration of these activities over strategic, tactical, and operational planning horizons (Shapiro, 2001).

In summary, Supply Chain Management (SCM) can be defined as the management of flows of goods between the different stages in a supply chain in order to minimize system-wide cost and satisfy customer requirements.

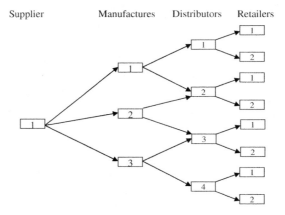

Figure 1.1: Four-stage supply chain network.

The supply chain is often represented as a network like the one displayed in Figure 1.1. The nodes in the network represent the firms or the supply chain partners. These nodes are connected by the transportation links that allow the flow of materials, the flow of information and the flow of cash across the chain. Figure 1.1 depicts a supply chain that has four stages, which are vendors, plants distributors and retailers.

1.2 Supply chain modeling

There are variety of supply chain models developed for varying supply chain management and planning objectives. Shapiro (2001) classified mathematical models developed for implementation and application in supply chain management into two main types: descriptive models and optimization models.

Descriptive models are created by modeling practitioners to better understand functional relationship in the supply chain. They include demand forecasting models, cost relationship model, resource utilization relationship models, and supply chain system simulation model. Optimization models are either prescriptive models or normative models. Prescriptive models support the decision making process in identifying a set of decisions that can enhance the supply chain performance. Normative models help in identifying norms that the company should strive (Shapiro, 2001).

1.3 Production-Inventory coordination in the supply chain

Supply chain production-inventory distribution coordination is a centralized planning process that deals with production lot-sizing, production scheduling, shipment quantities, and inventory allocation. In the centralized production and replenishment decision policy, the global supply chain costs are optimized. While in the decentralized production and replenishment decision policy, each participant within the supply chain will consider optimizing its own costs independently.

In recent years numerous articles in supply chain modeling have addressed the issue of inventory-distribution coordination. Several researchers focused on the integrated vendor-buyer inventory and the joint economic lot sizing problem models (see reviews by Ben-Daya et al. 2008; and Khouja and Goyal 2008). Other researchers suggested that the inventory-distribution coordination can be achieved by synchronization of the cycle time across the chain stages. In many cases, pure just-in-time (JIT) schedules using a common synchronized common production-replenishment cycle are found not to be optimal. Therefore other developed supply chain models achieve coordination by following the integer multipliers mechanisms in which the cycle time at each stage is an integer multiple of the cycle time of the adjacent downstream stage (Khouja, 2003).

1.4 Benefits of Inventory Coordination

The benefits of inventory coordination and information sharing among the supply chain participants, have received significant attention in the literature. Research findings in this area revealed that information sharing and coordinated

4

inventory replenishments can help reduce the inventory and order costs as well as transportation costs.

Lee et al. (1997) in their investigation on the bullwhip effect in supply chains reported that lack of information sharing can lead to excessive inventory, poor customer service, lost revenues, unplanned capacities, and ineffective logistics. They recommend avoiding managerial independence by integrating various supply chain functions. They also, recommend that firms need to device strategies that lead to smaller batches or frequent replenishments. Exchange of substantial quantities of information among the buyer, supplier, and carrier can increase the efficiency and effectiveness of the supply chain (Carter et al., 1995). Coordinated replenishment can significantly reduce inventory. Inventory reductions have a significant impact on supply chain activities. Lower inventory levels increase operating revenues and reduce the need for costly facilities (Esper and Williams, 2003).

Chen and Chen (2005) investigated the centralized, coordinated replenishment policy and the decentralized replenishment policy in a two-echelon, multi item supply chain. They determined the optimal common replenishment cycle for end items and the integer multiples of the common replenishment cycle for raw materials. They pointed out that a centralized, coordinated replenishment policy was always found to be superior to the decentralized replenishment policy in terms of cost reduction, especially when major setup costs were high.

Inventory coordination can also reduce other operations costs. For example, Collaborative transportation management in supply chain can significantly reduce the retailer's total costs and improve the retailer's service level (Chan and Zhang, 2011).

1.5 The Aim of this Book

In the past, supply chain production-inventory decisions were not coordinated and information was not shared among the different parties in the supply chain. This lack of coordination leads to weakly connected activities and decisions across the supply chain. Today, timely sharing and coordination of information across the supply chains in addition to the emerging electronic commerce capabilities have changed the way supply chains operate. The global visibility of production-inventory profiles across the supply chain leads to coordinated decisions and in turn to reduced costs and improved customer service.

In recent years, supply chain production and inventory coordination received a lot of attention. Most of the developed models deal with two-stage chains. Even when multi-stage supply chains are considered, most of the developed models are based on restrictive assumptions such as the deterministic demand. Therefore, there is a need to analyze models that relax the usual assumptions to allow for a more realistic analysis of the supply chain. This book extends previous work in the inventory coordination in multi-stage supply chains, and to address the following research questions:

  i.   How can the supply chain network configured for better coordination?
  ii.   How to develop algebraic models to drive the optimal replenishment policy for the multi-stage supply chain?
  iii. How can the benefits resulting from inventory coordination be shared among the supply chain partners?
  iv.   What is the effect of stochastic demand on modeling inventory coordination in multi-stage supply chains ?

The ultimate objective for this book is to develop mathematical optimization models that can be utilized to efficiently coordinate and integrate the production-inventory decisions among the supply chain partners. These partners are suppliers, manufactures, distributors/warehouses, and stores/retailers. However, such collaboration among the supply chain partners requires mutual trust and coordination benefit sharing scheme. Therefore, this book also aims to develop a benefit sharing scheme to entice the production-inventory coordination across the entire supply chain.

To achieve this objective a multi-stage, non-serial supply chain model will be formulated first, and then cost minimization procedures will be proposed to obtain feasible and satisfactory solutions to the problem. Subsidiary objectives to achieve this main objective include:

1. To develop mathematical models for the multi-stage supply chains. These models will take in to account different inventory coordination mechanism.
2. To develop a mathematical model that can be used to support supply chain strategic policy making such as network reconfiguration.
3. To develop a benefits sharing scheme.

1.6 The Scope of this Book

In this book we consider the case of a multi-stage supply chain where a firm can supply many customers. This supply chain system consists of suppliers, manufactures, distributors and retailers. The production rates for the suppliers and manufactures are assumed finite. In addition the demand for each firm is assumed to be stochastic. The problem is to coordinate production and inventory decisions across the supply chain so that the total cost of the system is minimized. The model is developed under the following assumptions:

(a) A single product is produced and distributed through a four stage, multi customer, non-serial , supply chain
(b) Production rates are deterministic and uniform
(c) Unsatisfied demands at the end retailers are backordered
(d) Ordering /setup costs are the same for firms at the same stage
(e) Holding costs cost are the same for firms at the same stage
(f) Shortage costs are the same for firms at the same stage
(g) A lot produced at stage is sent in equal shipments to the downstream stage.

1.7 Contributions of this Book

As mentioned earlier numerous articles in supply chain modeling have been written in response to the global competition. However, most of the developed supply chain inventory models deal with two-stage supply chains. Even when multi-stage supply chains are considered, most of the developed models are based on restrictive assumptions such as of the deterministic demand. But Supply chains are stochastic in nature. Therefore, there is a need to analyze models that relax the usual assumptions to allow for a more realistic analysis of the supply chain inventory coordination.

1.8   Structure of the book

This book on multi-stage supply chain inventory coordination is presented in eight chapters. The organization of the book is as follows: chapter 1 is dedicated to give brief introduction the supply chain management and inventory coordination, benefits of the coordination, the aim of the book, scope of the book, and organization of the book.

Chapter 2 provides a review of the research on supply chain inventory modeling. This review included contributions related to two stage supply chains as well as multi-stage supply chain models.

Chapter 3 presents the mathematical description of the problem and the methodology that the researcher used in this research work. It also describes the different inventory coordination mechanisms.

In chapter 4, selected   supply chain deterministic models are used to demonstrate the use of algebraic method to solve these kinds of supply chain inventory models.

Chapter 5 presents the development of an optimal replenishment policy using a simple algebraic method to solve the general n-stage, multi-customer, non-serial supply chain inventory problem.

In chapter 6, the modeling approach developed in chapter 4 and chapter 5 is applied the integrated supply chain inventory transportation model.

Chapter 7 describes a stochastic four-stage supply chain model and presents a solution procedure.

Chapter 8 summarizes this book, outlines the major contributions, and presents its conclusion remarks and recommendations for future research.

1.9 Summary

With the growing focus on supply chain management (SCM), firms realized the need to improve their cost efficiency through closer collaboration among the chain partners and through high level of coordination of various decisions. This efficient supply chain coordination requires that the flow of products and information among the supply chain members is managed in cooperative manner.

This book is dealing with the problem of coordinating production and inventory decisions across the multi-stage supply chain so that the total cost of the system is minimized. For this purpose, we develop mathematical models to deal with different inventory coordination mechanisms between the chain members.

Chapter 2

Overview of Supply Chain Inventory Coordination Models

2.1   Introduction

Recently numerous articles in supply chain modeling have been written in response to the global competition. The purpose of this chapter is to survey research on supply chain inventory coordination models.

The scope of this review will include contributions related to two stage supply chains as well as multi-stage supply chain models. Some of the authors used analytical modeling methods, while others used simulation modeling approaches. However, this main focus will be on analytical modeling methods. Some of the models are deterministic and others are stochastic.

2.2   Two Stage Models

Goyal (1976) developed an integrated model for a single supplier-single customer problem. This model assumes a uniform deterministic product demand with respect to time, infinite rate of production, no permission for stock outs at the customer's end and zero lead time for the supplier and customer. He assumed lot for lot policy in which the production lot size is equal to the shipment size. The economic inventory policy derived from the integrated model found to result in minimum joint variable costs for the supplier and the customer. But this policy increased the customer individual cost. Therefore, he proposed a scheme for allocating the variable cost to the supplier and the customer. The supplier needs to compensate the customer either by the proposed scheme or by offering a carefully chosen quantity discount scheme.

Banerjee (1986) introduced the concept of joint economic lot sizing problem (JELS). He considered the case of a single vendor and a single purchaser under the assumption of deterministic demand and lot for lot policy. His objective was to show that a joint optimal policy adopted through a spirit of cooperation can be of economic benefit to both parties. He relaxed the infinite production rate assumption of Goyal (1976). In addition, Banerjee analyzed the effects of each party's optimal lot size on the other in case of independent optimization and developed a JELS model that focused on the joint total relevant cost (JTRC). He also demonstrated the advantage of The JELS approach through an analysis of the cost tradeoffs from the perspective of every party's optimal position. The paper concluded that by adopting a jointly optimal ordering policy, one party's loss is more than offset by the gain of the other and the benefit can be shared among both parties in some equitable fashion.

Goyal & Szendrovits (1986) presented a constant lot size model where the lot is produced through a fixed sequence of manufacturing stages, with a single setup and without interruption at each stage. Transportation of partial lots, called batches, is allowed between stages. This model mainly, relaxes the constraint that batches must be of equal size at any particular stage. The model assumed deterministic demand and it is applicable to an unrestricted number of stages. They developed a procedure for determining the economic lot size and the batch sizes for each stage. They proved that generally costs resulting from the developed model are lower than the cost generated by the model that requires equal batch sizes at a particular stage. The setup costs are ignored in this model. Also the model assumes unrestricted production capacity.

Goyal and Gupta (1989) extensively reviewed the literature which deals with the interaction between a buyer and vendor. They classified the literature dealing with the integrated models into four main classes. The first class represents models which deal with joint economic lot sizing policies. The second class characterizes

11

models which deal with the coordination of inventory by simultaneously determining the order quantity for the buyer and the vendor. The third class is a group of models which deal with integrated problem but do not determine simultaneously the order quantity of the buyer and the vendor. The last class represents models which deal with buyer vendor coordination due to marketing considerations.

Lu (1995) developed a one-vender multi-buyer integrated inventory model with the objective of minimizing the vender's total annual cost subject to the maximum cost that the buyer may be prepared to incur. The model is appropriate when the vendor has the advantage over the buyer in the purchasing negotiation. Implementation of this model only requires that the vendor should know the buyer's annual demand and previous ordering frequency, which can be inferred from buyer's ordering history. Lu has found the optimal solution for the single-vendor single-buyer case under the stated assumptions and presented a heuristic approach for the one-vendor multi-buyer case. However, this model did not consider the case when the buyer tries to minimize total cost subject to minimum profits acceptable to the vendor.

Goyal (1995) revisited the single-vendor single-buyer where he relaxed the constraint of equal sized shipments of Goyal (1988) and suggested that the ratio between the sizes of each two successive shipments is equal to a fixed number n. This number is set to the ratio of vendor's production rate to the buyer's demand rate. This means the shipment size will grow geometrically. He used the numerical example of Lu (1995) to illustrate that a different shipment policy could give better solution. Hill (1997) considered a more general class of shipment policy for the single-vender, single buyer integrated production-inventory model. He generalized Goyal's (1995) model by taking the successive shipments to the buyer, within a single production batch, increasing by a geometric growth factor. Hill used the range starting form 1 up to the ratio of the production rate to the demand rate as the search range for the growth factor. In addition, the search range for the number of shipments is set to be from the optimal number of equal shipments for equal sized shipments policy to the optimal number of shipments of Goyal's (1995). Hill suggested a solution procedure which outperforms both the equal sized policy and Goyal's policy but does not guarantee a globally optimal solution to this problem.

Ha and Kim (1997) addressed the integration between the buyer and supplier for effective just-in-time (JIT) system. They developed an integrated lot splitting-model of facilitating multiple shipments in small lots. The developed model is then compared with the existing approach in a simple model of JIT, single vendor, single buyer for a single product under deterministic conditions. The result of their study showed that the optimal policy adopted by the integrated approach can provide a strong and consistent cost minimization effect for both parties over the simple model of JIT.

Viswanathan (1998) considered the integrated single-vendor single buyer model. Specifically, he considered the situation where a single vendor and buyer co-ordinate their production and inventory policies for the item that is produced and supplied by the vendor. He proposed two different strategies for this situation. The first is the identical delivery quantity (IDQ) strategy which is proposed by Lu. (1995). This strategy is an improvement over policies that were proposed by Banerjee(1986). The other strategy is called deliver what is produced' (DWP) strategy. According to this policy, the entire inventory available with the vendor is shipped to the buyer. Goyal's (1995) presented an example where DWP strategy outperforms the IDQ strategy. Viswanathan showed that neither strategy dominates the other for all possible problem parameters.

Hill (1999) discussed the single-vendor single-buyer integrated production-inventory problem with the objective of finding the optimal solution structure to the problem without any assumptions regarding the shipment policy. He showed that the optimal solution structure is a combination of the equal sized shipments policy and Goyal's (1995) policy. He proposed a relatively straightforward solution procedure. This model did not consider the case when there is delivery constraint on the maximum quantity which can be shipped at any time. Goyal (2000) extended the model of by Hill (1997) by increasing the following shipment sizes by the ratio of the production rate to the demand rate as long as it was feasible to do so. For the remaining shipments, the remaining part of the production run is distributed equally.

13

Goyal proved numerically with two examples that his results outperform the results obtained by applying Goyal's (1995) and Hill's (1997) methods.

Goyal and Nebebe (2000) considered the problem of determining economic production and shipment policy for a product supplied by a vendor to a single-buyer. They suggested a simple policy in which it is assumed that the batch quantity will be received by the buyer in n shipments. The first shipment will be of small size followed by $(n-1)$ equal sized shipment that equal to the ratio of the production rate to the demand rate multiplied by the first shipment size. This policy ensures a quick delivery of the first shipment to the buyer and avoids excessive inventory levels of higher order shipments at the buyer's end. The authors gave the optimal solution under this policy and showed that their policy outperforms Goyal's (1995), Lu's (1995) and Hill's (1997) policies.

Hoque and Goyal (2000) extended the idea of producing a single product in a multistage serial production system with equal and unequal sized batch shipments between stages. They assumed that batches are sent to the buyer in a number of equal and unequal shipments increasing by a fixed factor and the capacity of transport equipment used to transfer batches from vender to buyer is limited. The established a number of properties that the optimal solution must satisfy. The used these properties to develop an algorithm for determining the optimal policy.

Fu and Piplani (2004) addressed the approach to evaluate the supply-side collaboration by focusing on inventory decisions between the supplier and the distributor. They used two scenarios for comparison. First, a traditional scenario is considered where the distributor is unaware of the supplier's inventory decisions and no collaboration policy is followed. The other scenario involves the simple supply-side collaboration where the distributor is aware of the supplier's inventory policy(r, Q) and the planned service level as provided by the supplier. This work is limited only to the evaluation of the distributor's performance.

Lee (2005) considered a single-manufacturer single-supplier supply chain where the manufacturer orders its raw materials from its supplier, the converts the

14

raw materials into finished goods, and finally delivers the finished goods to its customers. He proposed an integrated inventory control model that comprises of integrated vendor-buyer (IVB) and integrated procurement-production (IPP) systems. The objective was to minimize the meant total cost per unit time of the raw materials ordering and holding, manufacturing setup and the finished goods holding, the buyer's ordering as well as its inventory holding.

Chen and Chen (2005) proposed a joint replenishment program coupled with a channel coordination practice, to investigate their effect on supply chain improvements. They formulated several supply chain models, with a manufacturer supplying a family of products to a retailer, and the products sharing a common production facility. The models illustrated the challenge of integrating multi-items with multi-echelon production and replenishment. In addition, they developed a saving-sharing mechanism, through a quantity discount scheme so that Pareto improvements (i.e., one party is better off and the other is no worse off) can be achieved among channel participants. Lee and Wu (2006) considered a simplified two-echelon supply chain system, with one supplier and one retailer that can choose different replenishment policies. They used two types of inventory replenishment methods: the traditional methods (the event-triggered and the time-triggered ordering policies), and the statistical process control (SPC) based replenishment method. Their results show that the latter outperforms the traditional method in the categories of inventory variation, and in the number of backlog when the fill-rate of the prior model is set to be 99%.

Dumrongsir et al. (2006) considered a dual channel supply chain in which a manufacturer sells to a retailer as well as to consumers directly. Consumers choose the purchase channel based on price and service qualities. The manufacturer decides the price of the direct channel and the retailer decides both price and order quantity. They developed conditions under which the manufacturer and the retailer share the market in equilibrium. Ertogral et al. (2007) analyzed the vendor–buyer lot sizing problem incorporating the transportation cost explicitly into their model. They used all-unit-discount structure with and without over declaration.

Wee and Chung (2007) used a simple algebraic method to solve the economic lot size of the integrated vendor–buyer inventory problem. As a result, a simple solution procedure is developed with ease. Hua and Li (2008) investigated how the retailer's sensitivity affects the retailer's dominance over the manufacturer in the cooperative and non-cooperative scenarios. They also analyzed impacts of demand uncertainty on retailer's dominance and supply chain cooperation.

Hoque (2008) considered the integrated single-vendor multi-buyer inventory problem. He developed three models, two of which transfer with equal batches (part of a lot) and the third with unequal batches of the product. He presented optimal solution techniques. His sensitivity analysis and comparative study of the results shows that the supply chain by unequal batches performs better. But solution techniques are simpler in the two cases with equal batches.

Sarmah et al. (2006) reviewed literature dealing with buyer vendor coordination models that have used quantity discount as coordination mechanism under deterministic environment and classified the various models. Kang and Kim (2010) developed heuristic algorithms by simultaneously considering inventory and transportation decisions for a single-supplier multi- retailers supply chain.

More recent reviews on the integrated vendor-buyer inventory and the joint economic lot sizing problem models can be found in   Ben-Daya et al. (2008); and Khouja and Goyal (2008).

2.3   Multi Stage Integrated Inventory Models

Khouja (2003) considered the case a three-stage supply where a firm can supply many customers and developed the model to deal with three inventory coordination mechanisms between the chain members. In the first mechanism all firms in the chain follow the same identical cycle times. The second mechanism is integer multiplier in which firms in the each stage of the supply chain use the same cycle time and the cycle time at each stage is an integer multiplier of the cycle time in the next downstream stage. The third mechanism is further generalization of the

16

integer multiplier cycle time inventory coordination mechanism, in which the cycle time is an integer power of two multiplier of a basic cycle time. In addition the powers of two at each firm are made equal or greater than the largest powers of two of any of the firm's customers at the adjacent downstream stage. He solved the cost minimization model for each mechanism. His results and numerical analysis showed that the integer multiplier coordination mechanism has lower total cost than the equal cycle time mechanism, and the integers powers of two multipliers has lower total cost than the integer multipliers mechanism. Khouja Model (2003) represents the most generic form of modeling the inventory coordination in the supply chain. Besides, it uses an easy modeling approach. For these two reasons we adopt this model as a grounding foundation for modeling the supply chain inventory coordination throughout this book.

Bendaya and Nassar (2008) relaxed the assumption of Khouja's (2003) regarding the completion of the whole production lot before making shipments out of it and assumed that equal sized shipments take place as soon as they are produced and there is no need to wait until a whole lot is produced. The presented model assumed vertically integrated production system in the sense that it is partially or jointly owned so that benefit sharing is not an issue. They have showed that their model has resulted in cost savings of about 11.50% compared to the model proposed by Khouja (2003).

Cárdenas-Barrón (2006) revisited the problem formulated by Khouja (2003) considering only the simplest inventory coordination mechanism which is referred to as the same cycle time for all companies in the supply chain. It was concluded that it is possible to use an algebraic approach to optimize the supply chain model without the use of differential calculus.

Chung and Wee (2007) considered an integrated three-stage inventory system with backorders. The formulated the problem to derive the replenishment policies with four-decision-variables algebraically. Chiu (2008) presented a simple algebraic method to demonstrate that the lot size solution and the optimal production-inventory cost of an imperfect EMQ model can be derived without derivatives. Kim and Park

(2008) developed a three-echelon supply chain empirical model to optimize the coordination costs.

Rau and OuYang (2008) presented an integrated production–inventory policy under a finite planning horizon and a linear trend in demand. They assumed that the vendor makes a single product and supplies it to a buyer with a non-periodic and just-in-time (JIT) replenishment policy in a supply chain environment. They first, developed a mathematical model and proved that it has the optimal solution. Then, they described an explicit solution procedure for obtaining the optimal solution and they provided two numerical examples to illustrate both increasing and decreasing demands in the proposed model.

Jaber and Rosen (2007) suggested the application of the first and second laws of thermodynamics to reduce system entropy, to improve production system performance. They postulated that the behavior of production systems very much resembles that of physical systems. They demonstrated applicability of these laws in a simple reverse supply chain context, where products are collected and later repaired at some rate while other products might be disposed outside according to some waste disposal rate.

Tsiakisa and Papageorgiou (2008) developed a mixed integer linear programming (MILP) model to determine the optimal configuration of a production and distribution network subject to operational and financial constraints. Operational constraints include quality, production and supply restrictions, and are related to the allocation of the production and the work-load balance. Financial constraints include production costs, transportation costs and duties for the material flowing within the network subject to exchange rates. As a business decision the out-sourcing of production is considered whenever the organization cannot satisfy the demand.

Nagarajan, M. and Sošić (2008) surveyed some applications of cooperative game theory to supply chain management. They first, described the construction of the set of feasible outcomes in commonly seen supply chain models, and then used cooperative bargaining models to find allocations of the profit pie between supply chain partners. They analyzed and surveyed several models. Then they discussed the issue of coalition formation among supply chain partners. Thy presented an exhaustive survey of commonly used stability concepts.

Pujaria et al (2008) developed an integrated inventory distribution optimization model that simultaneously incorporates the issues of location, production, inventory, and transportation within a supply chain. Their objective was to determine the optimal number and size of shipments under varying but commonly practiced production and shipping scenarios. They provided a continuous approximation procedure to determine the optimal number and size of shipments. They obtained closed form expressions for the optimal number of shipments for all the cases they analyzed.

Ding and Chen (2008) studied coordination issue of a three level supply chain selling short life cycle products in a single period model. The manufacturer first negotiates the trade contract with the retailer, then with the supplier. They construct the so-called flexible return policy by setting the rules of pricing while postponing the determination of the final contract prices. They showed that the three level supply chain can be fully coordinated with appropriate contracts and the total profit of the channel can be allocated with any specified ratios among the firms.

2.4   Stochastic Supply Chain Models

Lee and Kim (2002) proposed a framework of discrete-continuous combined modeling for supply chain simulation. Equations for the continuous aspects of a supply chain in this framework are included. The combined simulation modeling helps to observe the supply chain more macroscopically and to save the simulation execution times.   Weng and McClurg (2003) considered a two-party system in which the buyer orders from the supplier some quantity of a product to be used in production or resold directly to its customers. The buyer is faced with random demand over a selling period that has definite beginning and ending points. In addition, the delivery lead time of the supplier is uncertain. The primary objective was to investigate the benefits and limitations of information sharing and coordination in hedging   against demand and delivery time uncertainty, and to offer insights regarding the conditions under which information sharing and coordination

19

are most beneficial. The formulated expected profit models and derived results for the expected system profits with and without coordination on order quantity decisions.

Yao and Chiou (2004) considered an integrated supply chain model in which one vendor supplies items for the demand of multiple buyers. Their objective was to minimize the vendor's total annual cost subject to the maximum cost that the buyer may be prepared to incur. They explored the optimality structure of this integrated model and asserted that the optimal cost curve is piece-wise convex.

Mason et al. (2003) developed a discrete event simulation model of a multi-product supply chain to examine the potential benefits to be gained from global inventory visibility and integration of the warehouse and transportation functions.

Banerjee et al. (2003) used simulation to examine the effects of two lateral (intra-echelon) transshipment approaches in a two-echelon supply chain network. Santoso et al. (2005) developed a stochastic programming model for large-scale supply chain network design problem under uncertainty. They proposed a solution algorithm that integrates an accelerated decomposition scheme along with recently developed sampling average approximation (SAA) method. The proposed methodology provides an efficient framework for identifying and statistically testing a variety of candidate design solutions.

Long et al. (2005) studied a supply chain model in which a single supplier sells a single product to a single retailer who faces the newsvendor problem. The retailer is loss averse. The results showed that the optimal production quantity with decentralized decision making with a wholesale price contract is less than that with centralized decision making. The supply chain can achieve channel coordination with buy back and target rebate contracts. With buy back contracts, the supply chain system profits can be allocated arbitrarily between the supplier and retailer. A new kind of contract, the incremental buy back contract, gives similar results as with the buy back contract. The advantages and drawbacks of these three types of contracts were analyzed with numerical examples. Han (2005) established a strategic resource allocation model to capture and encapsulate the complexity of the modern global supply chain management problem. He constructed a mathematical model to describe the stochastic multiple-period two-echelon inventory with the many-to-many demand-supplier network problem. He applied Genetic algorithm (GA) to derive optimal solutions through a two-stage optimization process. His model simultaneously constitutes the inventory control and transportation parameters as well as price uncertainty factors.

Li and Liu (2006) developed a quantity discount model for a supplier–buyer system selling one type of product with multi-period and probabilistic customer demand. They showed that quantity discount policy is a way that may be implemented to achieve coordination. Their results illustrated that there is a bound of quantity discount in which both sides can accept and the increased profit due to joint decision can be measured using this bound. They also designed a method to divide it between the buyer and supplier, and obtained the optimal quantity discount policy by using this profit sharing method.

Barnes-Schuster et al. (2006) studied a system composed of a supplier and buyer(s).They assumed that the buyer faces random demand with a known distribution function. The supplier faces a known production lead time. Their main objective was to determine the optimal delivery lead time and the resulting location of the system inventory. For a system with a single-supplier and as single-buyer, they showed that system inventory should not be split between a buyer and supplier. They also derived the conditions indicating when the supplier or buyer(s) should keep the system inventory, based on systems parameters of shortage and holding costs, production lead times, and standard deviations of demand distributions.

Man-Yi and Xiao-Wo (2006) studied how to evaluate the safety stock of node enterprise given desired product availability when market demand of the node enterprise in supply chain is described by Gauss fuzzy variable. They discussed the impact of required product availability and demand uncertainty on safety stock, compared the correlative issues with stochastic demand, and got some useful results. Leung (2008) considered the EOQ problem, where the quantity backordered and the quantity received are both uncertain. They used complete squares method to derive a global optimal expression from a non-convex objective function in an algebraic manner. They presented a numerical example to illustrate the solution procedure.

Karabatı and Sayına (2008) addressed the coordination problem in a single-supplier/multiple-buyer supply chain with vertical information sharing, where the supplier wishes to coordinate the supply chain by offering quantity discounts to the buyers. They modeled each buyer's net savings expectations based on her limited view of the entire supply chain which consists of herself and the supplier only, and then incorporated these expectations into the modeling of the supply chain conducted by the supplier, which results in a constrained Stackelberg game. They considered both price discriminatory and non-price discriminatory approaches. Their numerical analysis of the coordination efficiency and allocation of the net savings of the proposed discount schemes showed that the supplier is still able to coordinate the supply chain with high efficiency levels, and retain a significant portion of the net savings.

El Saadanya and Jaber (2008) considered a centralized decision model for a two-level coordinated (manufacturer–retailer) to minimize the local costs and that of the chain. They developed mathematical models under the assumption of imperfect process where production may be interrupted to restore process quality. Farahania. and Elahipanaha developed and a model for just-in-time (JIT) distribution for the distribution network of a three-echelon supply chain, with two objective functions: minimizing costs, and minimizing the sum of backorders and surpluses of products in all periods. They assumed delivery lead times and capacity constraints in a multi-period, multi-product and multi-channel network. They developed hybrid genetic algorithm to solve real-size numerical examples.

Smitha et al. (2008) identified that majority of these simulation techniques rely upon a detailed market structure being known, when this is rarely the case and described how to develop of a pragmatic set of tools to gather, assess and verify supply chain structure data. A hybrid collection of technologies are utilized to assist these operations and to build a dynamic supply network model.

2.5 Summary

In this chapter the relevant reviewed literature is reviewed. The significant contributions in the development of the integrated supply chain modeling are highlighted. This review starts at few earliest models appeared after the mid seventies, and covers up the latest works in this area. In the reviewed literature, different models in supply chain production-inventory coordination are proposed. Some models are simple serial two stage models with deterministic demand and other few models are non-serial with three stages. The main objective considered in developing the models is to minimize the total cost. The methodologies followed to tackle the problem include: analytical, mathematical, optimization procedures and simulation tools. Several coordination mechanisms are proposed: equal shipment size, non-equal shipment size, integer multipliers and powers of two multipliers mechanisms.

This intensive literature review helped us in deeply understanding the problem on hand and highlighting the limitations of the previous work. The primary limitation of the work on inventory coordination for multi-stage supply chain is the assumption of deterministic uniform demand. It is noticeable that the general n-stage supply chain coordination has not been widely considered. Also models are not addressing the optimal network reconfiguration. Besides, the issue of sharing the coordination benefits resulting from coordinated inventory decisions is open for more research efforts. These four directions support and lead to this book.

Chapter 3

Inventory Coordination Modeling and Optimization Methods

3.1 Introduction

This chapter presents the research framework and research methodology. The research framework is detailed in section 3.1. Section 3.2 describes the research methodology.

3.2 Research Framework

The research framework followed this book consists of the elements depicted in Figure 3.1 below. In this research, the supply chain inventory coordination is addressed. The objective is to achieve a synchronized supply chain management via coordination. As shown in Figure 3.1, the synchronized supply chain management requires coordination across different functions and at the interfaces of the supply chain. The main focus of this research is on production and inventory coordination.

There are several mechanisms for inventory coordination proposed in the literature. Khouja (2003) presented three inventory coordination mechanisms between the chain members. In the first mechanism all firms in the chain follow the same identical cycle times. The second mechanism is integer multiplier in which firms in the each stage of the supply chain use the same cycle time and the cycle time at each stage is an integer multiplier of the cycle time in the next downstream stage. The third mechanism is further generalization of the integer multiplier cycle time inventory coordination mechanism, in which the cycle time is an integer power of two multiplier of a basic cycle time. In this book, mainly the integer multipliers inventory coordination mechanism is considered. This Mechanism is used to model multi-stage none-serial supply chains under deterministic and stochastic demands. Algebraic solution method is developed for the deterministic demand model. An optimization search algorithm can be used for the stochastic demand model.

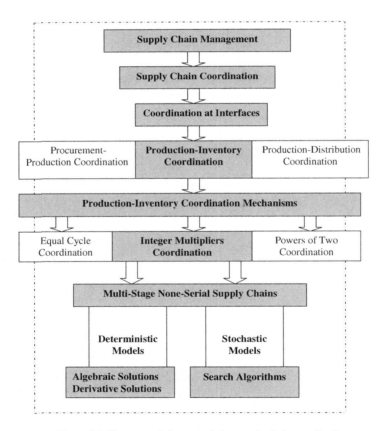

Figure 3.1: The research framework for supply chain coordination

3.3 The research Approach

The research methodology used to carry out this research is outlined in the following steps:

i. Define the problem.
ii. Mathematically formulate the models.
iii. Develop algebraic solution method for the deterministic models and local search based solution methods for the stochastic models.
iv. Perform sensitivity analysis.
v. Test and validate the models.

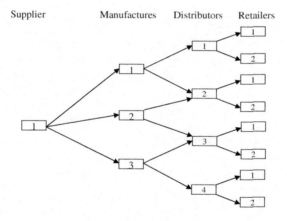

Figure 3.2: A typical complex supply chain structure

The following notations are used in developing the models:

T =Basic cycle time, cycle time at the end retailer
T_i =Cycle time at the stage i

A_i = Setup cost at stage i

K_i = Integer multiplier at stage i

h_i = Inventory holding cost at stage i

n_i = Number of firms at stage i

D_{ij} = The mean demand rate of firm j at stage i

P_{ij} = Production rate of firm j at stage i

$Av\_INVCost$ = The average inventory holding cost per unit time for the entire supply chain

$Av\_SHORTCost$ = The average shortage cost per unit time for the entire supply chain

$Av\_SetupCost$ = The average setup/order cost per unit time for the entire supply chain.

3.4 Mathematical Formulation

We assume the supply chain partners follow the integer multipliers inventory coordination mechanism in which firms at the same stage of the supply chain use the same cycle time and the cycle time at each stage is an integer multiplier of the cycle time used at the adjacent downstream stage. The formulation of the multi-stage, multi customers, non-serial supply chain according to this coordination mechanism is presented in the following subsection.

a. Integer –multiplier at each stage

When the supply chain model is formulated for the integer multipliers coordination mechanism, firms at the same stage of the supply chain use the same cycle time and the cycle time at each stage is an integer multiplier of the cycle time used at the adjacent downstream stage. Under this policy, the cycle time of an end retailer is T and we define the cost objective function $TC = f(T, K_1, K_2, K_3, ..., K_n)$ as:

$$f(T, K_1, K_2, K_3, ..., K_n) = Av\_INVCost + Av\_SHORTCost + Av\_SetupCost$$

The problem now can be stated in the following mathematical model

$$\text{MIN } TC = f(T, K_1, K_2, K_3, ..., K_n)$$

27

b. Integer Powers of two multipliers at each firm

The Powers of two multipliers policy is quite known in the literature of lot sizing problems (Yao and Elmaghraby, 2001, Ouenniche and Boctor, 2001). This policy requires that cycle time for each firm is made integer powers of two multiplier of a basic cycle time, and it allows firms within each stage to be unequal (Khouja, 2003). If there are g firms in the supply chain, then the problem now can be stated in the following general form

Defining $TC = f(T, K_1, K_2, ...K_g)$ as:

$$f(T, K_1, K_2, ...K_g) = Av\_INVCost + Av\_SHORTCost + Av\_SetupCost$$

The problem now can be stated in the following mathematical model

$$\text{MIN } TC = f(T, K_1, K_2, ..., K_g)$$

3.5 Algebraic Modeling Approach

The use of differential calculus to model the integrated production inventory systems is common in the area of operational research. However, several researchers focused on the easy solution methods for the optimization of these types of systems. For example Grubbström (1995) introduced the use of algebraic optimization approach to the EOQ model with no backorders. Since then, algebraic approach for the optimization of production inventory models has received considerable attention mathematics Cárdenas-Barrón(2011). Cárdenas-Barrón(2007) reviewed the algebraic procedure used by different researchers between (1995) and (2006) to solve the inventory problem. He classified this procedure according to its difficulty level as simple, medium and high. Again Cárdenas-Barrón(2011) conducted literature review on the use of algebraic optimization methods in the development of production inventory systems.

Cárdenas-Barrón (2001) used algebraic procedure to the EPQ formula taking shortages into consideration within the case of only one backlog cost per unit and time unit. Cárdenas-Barrón (2007) formulated and solved an n-stage-multi-customer

28

supply chain inventory model where there is a company that can supply products to several customers. The production and demand rates were assumed constant and known. This model was formulated for the simplest inventory coordination mechanism which is referred to as the same cycle time for all companies in the supply chain. It was concluded that it is possible to use an algebraic approach to optimize the supply chain model without the use of differential calculus. Chung and Wee (2007) considered an integrated three-stage inventory system with backorders. They formulated the problem to derive the replenishment policies with four-decision-variables algebraically. Wee and Chung (2007) also used a simple algebraic method to solve the economic lot size of the integrated –buyer inventory problem. As a result, students who are unfamiliar with calculus may be able to understand the solution procedure with ease. Chi (2008) presented a simple algebraic method to demonstrate that the lot size solution and the optimal production-inventory cost of an imperfect EMQ model can be derived without derivatives. Leung (2008) considered the EOQ problem, where the quantity backordered and the quantity received are both uncertain. He used the complete squares method to derive a global optimal expression from a non-convex objective function in an algebraic manner. Cárdenas-Barrón (In Press) considered the problem of optimal manufacturing batch size with rework process at single-stag production system. He determined the optimal solution for two different inventory policies. He also established the range of real values of proportion of defectives products for which there is an optimal solution, the closed-form for the total inventory cost for both policies, the mathematical expressions for determining the cost penalty and the additional total cost for working with a non-optimal solution.

Seliaman and Ahmad(2009) developed a more generalized inventory coordination model for an n-stage, multi-customer, non-serial supply chain. They extended and generalized pervious works that use algebraic methods to optimize this coordinated supply chain. They established the recursive expressions for this multi-variable optimization problem. These expressions were used for the derivation of the optimal replenishment policy and the development of the solution algorithm. Ben-Daya et al.(2010) considered the joint economic lot sizing problem (JELP) in the context of a three stage supply chain to specify the timings and quantities of inbound and outbound logistics for all parties involved such that the chain-wide total ordering, setup, raw material and finished product inventory holding costs are minimized. In Their model, the cycle time at each stage is set to be an integer multiple of that for the adjacent downstream stage. To bear a better resemblance to practice, shipments from a particular lot are allowed to take place during production and not after producing the whole lot. They employed derivative-free methods to derive a near closed form solution for the developed model. Leung (2010) generalized a number of integrated models with/without lot streaming under the integer multiplier coordination mechanism by allowing lot streaming and three types of inspection for some/all upstream firms. He developed the optimal solutions to the three- and four-stage models using a simple algebraic approach. He also presented two numerical examples for illustrative purposes and corrected the results of the numerical example in Seliaman and Ahmad (2009).

3.6 Summary

In this chapter we presented the elements of the general modeling framework used in this book. Then the mathematical description of the problem and the methodology that the researcher used in this book are outlined. Basically, two modeling and optimization approaches are considered. Next chapter will present some extended deterministic models.

Chapter 4

Algebraic Optimization of Some Selected Supply Chain Inventory Models

4.1 Introduction

The use of differential calculus to model the integrated production inventory systems is common in the area of operational research. However, several researchers focused on easier solution methods for the optimization of these types of systems. For example, Grubbström (1995) introduced the use of algebraic optimization approach to the EOQ model with no backorders. Since then, algebraic approach for the modeling and optimization of production inventory systems has received notable attention from researchers (Cárdenas-Barrón 2011). In this chapter, selected supply chain deterministic models are used to demonstrate the use of algebraic method to solve these kinds of models.

4.2 Reconfiguring the Network for Better Coordination

The configuration of the manufacturing and distribution facilities, and selection of distribution channels are typical strategic supply chain decisions. Ab Rahman and Seliaman (2007) considered the problem of reconfiguring the supply chain network to significantly improve customer service levels and reduce system wide cost. They developed a mathematical model that can help in the integrated design of strategic supply chain networks. The model was used to reconfigure the network of the supply chain example presented in Khouja (2003).

Numerical analysis revealed that under the new configuration and using equal cycle time mechanism, the total cost can be reduced by of 23% of the cost under the configuration in Khouja (2003). Under the new configuration and using integer multipliers mechanism, a saving of 35.8 % can be achieved. In this section we consider the problem of reconfiguring the supply chain network to significantly improve customer service levels and reduce system wide cost. For this purpose we develop a mathematical model that can help in the integrated design of strategic supply chain networks. In this model, inventory and production cycles are assumed synchronized across the entire supply chain. Under the new configuration, a firm can supply any customer in the adjacent downstream stage.

Notation

In addition to the notations stated in the previous chapters, the following notations are needed for the models developed in this chapter:

$$P_i = \sum_j P_{ij}$$ represents the total production rate at stage i

$$A_i = \sum_j A_{ij}$$ represents the total setup cost at stage i

$$D_i = \sum_j D_{ij}$$ represents the total demand rate at stage i

$$TC = \sum_{ij} TC_{ij}$$ represents total cost for the entire supply chain

4.2.1   Equal Cycle Time Coordination

Under this mechanism, all firms in the supply chain use the same cycle time. At an end retailer j, the inventory decreases with a rate of D_{4j} starting from $D_{4j}T$ as shown in figure 4.1. Therefore, the inventory holding cost per unit time for an end retailer is $\dfrac{TD_{4,j}h_4}{2}$.

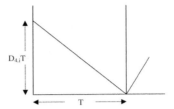

Figure 4.1: Inventory level at an end retailer

Since all retailers share the same cycle time, the total inventory holding cost per unit time at the fourth stage (retailers) is $h_4 T \sum_j \frac{D_{4,j}}{2}$ which is equal to $\frac{TDh_4}{2}$. Hence, the total cost per unit time at the fourth stage (retailers) can be formulated as:

$$TC_4 = \frac{TDh_4}{2} + \frac{A_4}{T}$$

(4.1)

The total cost per unit time for the distributors:

$$TC_3 = \frac{TDh_3}{2} + \frac{A_3}{T}$$

(4.2)

The first term of Equation (4.2) is the cost of holding finished goods received from the manufacturers' stage without any further processing.

The total cost for manufacturers is:

$$TC_2 = \frac{TD^2}{2P_2}(h_1 + h_2) + \frac{A_2}{T}$$

(4.3)

Similarly the total cost for the suppliers is:

$$TC_1 = \frac{TD^2}{2P_1}(h_0 + h_1) + \frac{A_1}{T}$$

(4.4)

The total cost of the whole supply chain is:

$$TC = \frac{T}{2}\left(\frac{D^2}{P_1}(h_0 + h_1) + \frac{D^2}{P_2}(h_1 + h_2) + D(h_3 + h_4)\right) + \frac{1}{T}((A_1 + A_2 + A_3 + A_4))$$

(4.5)

Rewriting equation (4.5), one has

$$TC = TY + \frac{W}{T}$$

(4.6)

Where

$$Y = \frac{\left(\dfrac{D^2}{P_1}(h_0 + h_1) + \dfrac{D^2}{P_2}(h_1 + h_2) + D(h_3 + h_4)\right)}{2}$$

And

$$W = \left(A_1 + A_2 + A_3 + A_4\right)$$

Now applying the algebraic procedure proposed by Cárdenas-Barrón (2007), the annual total cost for the entire supply chain in Eq. (4.6) can be represented by factorizing the term $1/T$ and completing the perfect square, one has

$$TC = \frac{1}{T}\left(T^2 Y - 2T\sqrt{YW} + W + 2T\sqrt{YW}\right)$$

(4.7)

Factorizing the perfect squared trinomial in a squared binomial we obtain:

$$TC = \frac{1}{T}\left(T\sqrt{Y} - \sqrt{W}\right)^2 + 2\sqrt{YW}$$

(4.8)

It is worthy pointing out that Eq. (4.8) reaches minimum with respect to T when setting

$$\left(T\sqrt{Y} - \sqrt{W}\right)^2 = 0$$

Hence, the optimal basic cycle time T^* is

$$T^* = \sqrt{\frac{W}{Y}}$$

(4.9)

Substituting Eq. (4.9) into Eq.(4.8), the minimum value for the annual total cost for the entire supply chain minimum cost is

$$TC = \sqrt{2\left(\frac{D^2}{P_1}(h_0 + h_1) + \frac{D^2}{P_2}(h_1 + h_2) + D(h_3 + h_4)\right)\left(A_1 + A_2 + A_3 + A_4\right)}$$

4.2.2 Integer Multipliers

For the integer multipliers coordination mechanism, the total cost per unit time for retailer's stage is given by the same expression (4.1) in the previous subsection. This is because retailers follow the same basic cycle time T.

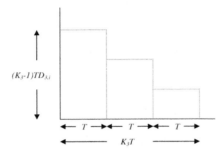

Figure 4.2: Inventory level at a distributor

For a distributor j at stage three, the inventory drops every T units of time starting from $(K_3-1)TD_{3,j}$ as shown in Figure 4.2. Therefore, the inventory holding cost per unit time for this distributor is $\dfrac{(K_3-1)h_3TD_{3,j}}{2}$. Since all distributors share the same cycle time, the total inventory holding cost per unit time at the third stage (distributors) is $\dfrac{(K_3-1)h_3}{2}\sum_j D_{3,j}$ which is equal to $\dfrac{(K_3-1)h_3TD_3}{2}$. Therefore, the total cost per unit time for all of the distributors:

$$TC_3 = \frac{(K_3-1)h_3TD_3}{2} + \frac{A_3}{K_3T} \qquad (4.9)$$

The total cost for the manufacturers is exactly as in Khouja (2003) and is given by:

$$TC_2 = \frac{K_2K_3TD_2^2h_1}{2P_2} + \frac{K_3TD_2}{2}(K_2(1+D_2/P_2)-1)h_2 + \frac{A_2}{K_2K_3T} \qquad (4.10)$$

Similarly the total cost for the suppliers is:

35

$$TC_1 = \frac{K_1 K_2 K_3 TD^2 h_0}{2P_1} + \frac{K_2 K_3 TD}{2}(K_1(1 + D_{1,j}/P_{1,j}) - 1)h_1 + \frac{A_1}{K_1 K_2 K_3 T} \quad (4.11)$$

To get the optimal cycle time T, we take the first derivative of the total annual cost of the entire supply chain $TC = \sum_{ij} TC_{ij}$ and solve $\partial TC/\partial T = 0$

$$T = \sqrt{\frac{2(A_1 + A_2 K_1 + A_3 K_1 K_2 + A_4 K_1 K_2 K_3)}{K_1 K_2 K_3 (\gamma D + \alpha \frac{D^2}{P_1} + \beta \frac{D^2}{P_2})}} \quad (4.12)$$

where $\gamma = (h_4 - h_3 + K_3(h_3 - h_2) + K_2 K_3(h_2 - h_1) + K_1 K_2 K_3 h_1)$,
$\beta = K_1 K_2 K_3 (h_0 + h)$ and $\alpha = K_2 K_3 (h_1 + h_2)$.
To minimize TC, the solution to $dTC/\partial K_1 = 0$ gives:

$$K_1 = \frac{1}{TK_2 K_3} \sqrt{\frac{2A_1}{\left(\frac{D^2 h_0}{P_1} + Dh_1 + \frac{D^2 h_1}{P_1}\right)}} \quad (4.13)$$

Substituting for K_1 from Eq. (4.13) back into TC, and the solving $\partial TC/\partial K_2 = 0$ gives:

$$K_2 = \frac{1}{K_3 T} \sqrt{\frac{2A_2}{\left(\frac{D^2}{P_2}(h_1 + h_2) + D(h_2 - h_1)\right)}} \quad (4.14)$$

The solution to $dTC/\partial K_3 = 0$ gives:

$$K_3 = \frac{1}{T} \sqrt{\frac{2A_3}{D(h_3 - h_2)}} \quad (4.15)$$

Substituting from (4.13), (4.14) and (4.15) back into TC, and the solving
$\partial TC/\partial T = 0$ gives:

$$T = \sqrt{\frac{2A_4}{D(h_4 - h_3)}} \quad (4.16)$$

36

This procedure is an extended version of the one in Khouja (2003).

4.2.3 Numerical Example

In this section, we consider an example of four -stage supply chain having one supplier, three manufacturers, six distributors, and seven retailers. The data for this example is shown in Table 4.1.

In this example setup cost is assumed to be highest at early stages of the chain, because these firms have complex and costly setups to process natural raw material. Then it becomes smaller at down stream stages (Khouja, 2003). The holding cost increases from early stages to late stages because of the value added. We used the same production and demand rates used by Khouja (2003) at the suppliers and manufacturers. The ratios of demand rates to demand rates are nearly in the range of 2-3.5.

Table 4.1: The data for the four-stage supply chain

	j	Set up cost	Holding cost	Demand	Production rate
Retailers	1	100	10	10,000	
	2	100	10	20,000	
	3	100	10	40,000	
	4	100	10	12,000	
	5	100	10	24,000	
	6	100	10	9,000	
	7	100	10	18,000	
Distributors	1	200	7	30,000	
	2	200	7	40,000	
	3	200	7	12,000	
	4	200	7	24,000	
	5	200	7	9,000	
	6	200	7	18,000	
Manufacturers	1	600	(0.8,1.5)	70,000	140,000
	2	600	(0.8,1.5)	36,000	108,000
	3	600	(0.8,1.5)	27,000	108,000
Suppliers	1	800	(0.08,0.8)	133,000	399,000

For this example under the equal cycle time mechanism, the optimal basic cycle time is 0.0479 years, and the total cost is TC=$71,015.541. While under the integer multipliers mechanism, the optimal basic cycle time at retailers' stage is 0.0220, and the optimal integer multipliers at the distributors, manufacturers and suppliers stages are equal to 1, 3, and 2 respectively. In this case, the total cost drops by 18.8% (from the cost when using equal cycle time mechanism) to TC=$57664.2254.

4.2.4   Sensitivity Analysis

We perform some sensitivity analysis on saving from using integer multipliers mechanism over the equal time cycle mechanism. We first decrease the current values of the setup cost at the suppliers, distributors, and manufacturers stages to 30%, 50% and finally 75% of the values in Table 4.1. The results are given in Table 4.2. We then increase the values of (h_0, h_1, and h_2) by using multipliers of (1.25, 1.50 and 2.00) of the original values. The results are presented in Table 4.3.

Table 4.2: Sensitivity analysis when (A_1, A_2, A_3) are decreased

(A_1,A_2,A_3) Decrease	30%		50%		75%	
	T*	ETC*	T*	ETC*	T*	ETC*
Equal time cycle	0.028	41480.40	0.035	51671.40	0.042	62101.28
Integer multipliers	0.017	36313.77	0.021	43751.88	0.024	51562.09
Saving	-	5166.63	-	7919.52	-	10539.19
% Saving	-	12.46	-	15.33	-	16.97

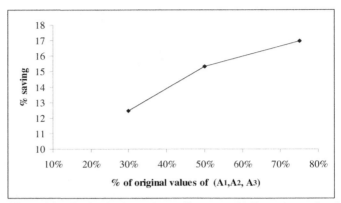

Figure 4.4: % Savings in the total cost of integer multipliers over equal cycle

Table 4.3: Sensitivity analysis when (h_0, h_1, and h_2) are increased

(h_0, h_1, and h_2) multipliers	1.25		1.50		2.00	
	T*	ETC*	T*	ETC*	T*	ETC*
Equal time cycle	0.0473	71927.11	0.0467	72827.27	0.0456	74595.00
Integer multipliers	0.0262	61006.87	0.0252	63565.76	0.0357	70790.46
Saving	-	10920.24		9261.51	-	3804.54
% Saving	-	15.18	-	12.72	-	5.10

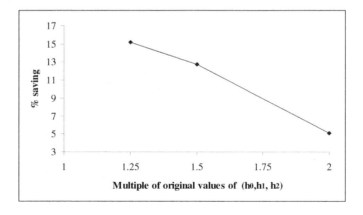

Figure 4.5: % Savings in the total cost of integer multipliers over equal cycle

Results presented in Table 4.2 and Figure 4.4 show that if setup cost is decreased at upstream stages, then the saving from using integer multipliers mechanism over the equal time cycle mechanism will decrease. From Table 4.3 and Figure 4.5 it can be concluded that if holding cost is increased at upstream stages, then the saving from using integer multipliers mechanism over the equal time cycle mechanism will decrease.

4.3   Multi-Stage Supply with Planned Back Orders

Consider the case of a four-stage supply chain where a firm can supply many customers with a single product. This supply chain system involves suppliers, manufactures, distributer and retailers. Production and inventory decisions are made at the suppliers and manufactures levels. The production rates for the suppliers and manufactures are assumed finite. In addition the demand for each firm is assumed to be deterministic. Unsatisfied demands at the end retailers are backordered. The problem is to coordinate production and inventory decisions across the supply chain so that the total cost of the system is minimized.

4.3.1   Assumptions and Notations

The following notations are used in developing the model:

T =Basic cycle time, cycle time at the end retailer

T_i =Cycle time at stage i

S_i =Setup cost at stage i

K_i =Integer multiplier at stage i

h_i =Inventory holding cost at stage i

D =The demand rate at the end stage

P_i=Production rate at stage i

π = Backordering cost per unit per unit time

Assumptions for the multi-stage supply chain production-inventory model:

(a)   A single product is produced and distributed through a four-stage serial, supply chain.

      (b)   Shortages are allowed for the end retailer.

      (c)   Replenishment is instantaneous.

      (d)   Production rates and Demand rate are deterministic and uniform.

      (e)   A lot produced at stage is sent in equal shipments to the downstream stage.

      (f)   The entire supply chain optimization is acceptable for all partners in the chain.

      (g)   Complete information sharing policy is adopted.

      (h)   Cycle time at each stage is an integer multiplier of the cycle time used at the adjacent downstream stage

4.3.2   Model Development

The retailer's cost consists of the inventory holding cost, the shortage cost and the setup cost. In this case as we can see from Fig. 1, the time-weighted total cost for the retailer is given by:

$$TC_4 = h_4 \frac{TD_4}{2} - T_S Dh_4 + h_4 \frac{T_S^2 D}{2T} + \pi \frac{T_S^2 D}{2T} + \frac{S_4}{T} \qquad (4.17)$$

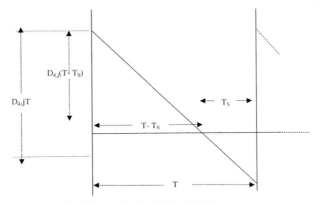

Fig.1. The inventory level at the end retailer

41

The inventory profiles at the remaining upstream stages are depicted by Figure 2. The inventory holding at each stage, except for the final stage (the end retailer at stage 4), is made of two parts: the first one is the carrying inventory of raw materials as they are being converted into finished products during the production portion of the cycle. The second part is the carrying inventory of the finished products during the non-production portion of the cycle Khouja [14]. Therefore, the total time-weighted cost for each of third, second, and first stages is represented by following equations respectively:

$$TC_3 = K_3 \frac{TD^2}{2P_3}(h_2 + h_3) + (K_3 - 1)\frac{TD}{2}h_3 + \frac{S_3}{K_3 T} \qquad (4.18)$$

$$TC_2 = K_2 K_3 \frac{TD^2}{2P_2}(h_1 + h_2) + K_3(K_2 - 1)\frac{TD}{2}h_2 + \frac{S_2}{K_2 K_3 T} \qquad (4.19)$$

$$TC_1 = K_1 K_2 K_3 \frac{TD^2}{2P_1}(h_0 + h_1) + K_2 K_3(K_1 - 1)\frac{TD}{2}h_1 + \frac{S_1}{K_1 K_2 K_3 T} \qquad (4.20)$$

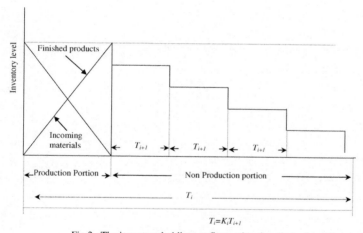

$$T_i = K_i T_{i+1}$$

Fig.2. The inventory holdings at firms other than the end retailer .

The entire supply time-weighted cost is

$$TC = \sum_{i,j} TC_{i,j} =$$

$$\frac{T}{2}\left\{\begin{array}{l} Dh_4 - Dh_3 + \\[4pt] K_3\left[\dfrac{D^2}{P_3}(h_2 + h_3) + Dh_3 - Dh_2\right] + \\[8pt] K_3K_2\left[\dfrac{D^2}{P_2}(h_1 + h_2) + Dh_2 - Dh_1\right] + \\[8pt] K_3K_2K_1\left[\dfrac{D^2}{P_1}(h_0 + h_1) + Dh_1\right] + \end{array}\right\} +$$

$$\frac{1}{T}\left\{S_4 + \frac{S_3}{K_3} + \frac{S_2}{K_2K_3} + \frac{S_1}{K_1K_2K_3}\right\} +$$

$$\frac{D(h_4 + \pi)}{2T}\left\{T_S^2 - \frac{2T_S h_4 T}{h_4 + \pi}\right\}$$

Now by using the method of completing square with respect to TS as in Chung and Wee [8], equation (5) can be rewritten as

$$TC = \frac{T}{2}\left\{\begin{array}{l} Dh_4 - Dh_3 - \dfrac{Dh_4^2}{h_4 + \pi} + \\[8pt] K_3\left[\dfrac{D^2}{P_3}(h_2 + h_3) + Dh_3 - Dh_2\right] + \\[8pt] K_3K_2\left[\dfrac{D^2}{P_2}(h_1 + h_2) + Dh_2 - Dh_1\right] + \\[8pt] K_3K_2K_1\left[\dfrac{D^2}{P_1}(h_0 + h_1) + Dh_1\right] + \end{array}\right\} +$$

$$\frac{1}{T}\left\{S_4 + \frac{S_3}{K_3} + \frac{S_2}{K_2K_3} + \frac{S_1}{K_1K_2K_3}\right\} +$$

$$\frac{D(h_4 + \pi)}{2T}\left\{T_S - \frac{h_4 T}{h_4 + \pi}\right\}^2 \qquad (4.21)$$

Rewriting equation (4.21), one has

$$TC = TY + \frac{W}{T} + \frac{D(h_4 + \pi)}{2T}\left\{T_S - \frac{h_4 T}{h_4 + \pi}\right\}^2 \qquad (4.22)$$

Where

$$Y = \frac{K_3\psi_3 + \alpha_3}{2}$$

$$\alpha_3 = Dh_4 - Dh_3 - \frac{h_4^2}{h_4 + \pi}$$

$$\psi_3 = K_2\psi_2 + \alpha_2$$

$$\alpha_2 = \frac{D^2}{P_3}(h_2 + h_3) + Dh_3 - Dh_2$$

$$\psi_2 = K_1\psi_1 + \alpha_1$$

$$\alpha_1 = \frac{D^2}{P_2}(h_1 + h_2) + Dh_2 - Dh_1$$

$$\psi_1 = \frac{D^2}{P_1}(h_0 + h_1) + Dh_1$$

$$W = \left(S_4 + \frac{\varphi_3}{K_3}\right)$$

$$\varphi_3 = \left(S_3 + \frac{\varphi_2}{K_2}\right)$$

$$\varphi_2 = \left(S_2 + \frac{S_1}{K_1}\right)$$

Now applying the algebraic procedure proposed by Cárdenas-Barrón(2007), the annual total cost for the entire supply chain in Eq. (4.22) can be represented by factorizing the term   and completing the perfect square, one has

$$TC = \frac{1}{T}\left(T^2Y - 2T\sqrt{YW} + W + 2T\sqrt{YW}\right) \qquad (4.23)$$
$$+ \frac{D(h_4 + \pi)}{2T}\left\{T_S - \frac{h_4T}{h_4 + \pi}\right\}$$

Factorizing the perfect squared trinomial in a squared binomial we obtain:

$$TC = \frac{1}{T}\left(T\sqrt{Y} - \sqrt{W}\right)^2 + \qquad (4.24)$$
$$\frac{D(h_4 + \pi)}{2T}\left\{T_S - \frac{h_4T}{h_4 + \pi}\right\} + 2\sqrt{YW}$$

It is worthy pointing out that Eq. (4.24) reaches minimum with respect to T and T_S when setting:

$$\left(T\sqrt{Y} - \sqrt{W}\right)^2 = 0$$

and

$$\left\{T_S - \frac{h_4T}{h_4 + \pi}\right\} = 0$$

Hence, the optimal basic cycle time T^* is

$$T^* = \sqrt{\frac{W}{Y}}$$

(4.25)

and the optimal allowable stocking out time T_S^* is

$$T_S^* = \frac{h_4}{h_4 + \pi} T^*$$

(4.26)

Substituting Eq. (4.25) and Eq. (4.26) into Eq.(4,24), the minimum value for the annual total cost for the entire supply chain is

$$TC = 2\sqrt{YW}$$

(4.27)

The optimal basic cycle time T^* is a function of the integer multipliers (K_3, K_2, K_1). We use the method of perfect square to drive the optimal values of these integer multipliers iteratively. Substituting for Y and W into Eq.(4.27) we get:

$$TC = \sqrt{2} \left\{ (K_3 \psi_3 + \alpha_3) \left(S_4 + \frac{\varphi_3}{K_3} \right) \right\}^{\frac{1}{2}} =$$

$$\sqrt{2} \left\{ \frac{1}{K_3} \left[K_3 \sqrt{\psi_3 S_4} - \sqrt{\alpha_3 \varphi_3} \right]^2 + \left[\sqrt{\psi_3 \varphi_3} + \sqrt{\alpha_3 S_4} \right]^2 \right\}^{\frac{1}{2}}$$

(4.28)

From (4.28) setting

$$\left[K_3 \sqrt{\psi_3 S_4} - \sqrt{\alpha_3 \varphi_3} \right]^2 = 0$$

the optimal value of integer multiplier K_3 is derived as follows:

$$(K_3^*).(K_3^* - 1) \le (K_3^*)^2 \le (K_3^*).(K_3^* + 1)$$

(4.29)

To drive the optimal value of integer multiplier K_2, we can rewrite the term $\sqrt{\psi_3 \varphi_3}$ in Eq. (4.28) as follows:

$$\sqrt{\psi_3 \varphi_3} = \left\{ \frac{1}{K_2} \left[K_2 \sqrt{\psi_2 S_3} - \sqrt{\alpha_2 \varphi_2} \right]^2 + \left[\sqrt{\psi_2 \varphi_2} + \sqrt{\alpha_2 S_3} \right]^2 \right\}$$

(4.30)

From Eq.(4.30) , setting

$$\left[K_2 \sqrt{\psi_2 S_3} - \sqrt{\alpha_2 \varphi_2} \right]^2 = 0$$

And the optimal value of the integer multiplier is derived as follows:

$$K_2^* = \sqrt{\frac{\alpha_2 \varphi_2}{\psi_2 S_3}}$$

(4.31)

Since the value K_2 of is a positive integer, the following condition must be satisfied:

$$(K^*_2).(K^*_2 - 1) \le (K^*_2)^2 \le K^*_2).(K^*_2 + 1) \tag{4.32}$$

Similarly, the optimal value of the integer multiplier K_1 is reached:

$$K^*_1 = \sqrt{\frac{\alpha_1 S_1}{\psi_1 S_2}} = \sqrt{\frac{[D(h_1 + h_2)/P_2 + h_2 - h_1]S_1}{[D(h_0 + h_1)/P_1 + h_1]S_2}} \tag{4.33}$$

Since the value of K_1 is a positive integer, the following condition must be satisfied:

$$(K^*_1).(K^*_1 - 1) \le (K^*_1)^2 \le K^*_1).(K^*_1 + 1) \tag{4.34}$$

Now, we can use K^*_1 to find K^*_2 which can be used to find K^*_3.

4.3.3 Numerical results

In this section, we consider an example of a four-stage supply chain consisting of a supplier, a manufacturer, a distributor, and a retailer. This example was originated by Goyal [7] for only two stages and was later extended by Chung and Wee [8] to include a distributor stage. To illustrate the model presented here in this paper, we added a supplier stage to the example. The relevant data is shown in Table 1. In addition to this data, backordering cost per unit per unit time is assumed 20. It is also assumed that holding cost for the supplier's supplier is $h_0=0.5$.

In this section, we consider an example of a three stage supply chain having one supplier, one manufacturer, and four retailers. The relevant data is shown in Table 4.12.

Table 4.10: Example data

i	P_i	D	h_i	S_i
1	4000	1000	2	650
2	3200	1000	4	400
3	2500	1000	4.2	40
4	-	1000	5	25

By applying the developed algebraic solution procedure in section 3, the results of this example are presented in Table 2. The optimal production lot size for the supplier is 816.07 which will be delivered to the manufacturer in two deliveries.

46

The optimal production lot size for the manufacturer is 408.04 which will be delivered to the distributor in three batches. However, the distributor and the retailer will share the same cycle length and the optimal batch size delivered by the distributor to the retailer is 136.01.

Table 4.11: Results for the example

Parameter	Solution
K_1	2
K_2	3
K_3	1
T	0.136
T_s	0.019
TC	5409.39

4.4   Summary

In this chapter we extended some of the reviewed deterministic models before developing the stochastic models.

First, a mathematical model for the strategic configuration/reconfiguration of the supply chain networks for better coordination is developed. The model is developed for three inventory coordination mechanisms.

Second, the inventory coordination when planned backorders are accepted is considered. A model is developed for this case and a procedure to obtain the optimal basic replenishment cycle and shortage duration is developed.

Chapter 5

The Generalized Algebraic Modeling of Supply Chain Inventory Coordination

5.1 Introduction

The use of differential calculus to model the integrated production inventory systems is common in the area of operational research. However, several researchers focused on the easy solution methods for the optimization of these types of systems. Cárdenas-Barrón (2006), Wee and Chung (2007), Chi (2008), and Leung (2008) are examples of models that use simple algebraic methods to optimize the supply chain production and inventory decisions without the use of differential calculus. In this chapter, we develop an optimal replenishment policy using a simple algebraic method to solve the general n-stage, multi-customer, non-serial supply chain inventory problem. Our work is an extension of the three stage supply chain model in Khouja (2003). The equal cycle inventory coordination case was modeled algebraically by Cárdenas-Barrón (2006). Hence we only need to consider the integer multiplier coordination mechanism.

5.2 Algebraic Modeling of the Supply Chain Inventory

We consider a multi-stage, non-serial supply chain, where a firm at each stage can have two or more customers. This supply chain model is formulated for the integer multipliers coordination mechanism, where firms at the same stage of the supply chain use the same cycle time and the cycle time at each stage is an integer multiplier of the cycle time used at the adjacent downstream stage. In this case, the cycle time of an end retailer is T and therefore the total cost per unit time for retailer j is given by:

$$TC_{n,j} = h_n \frac{TD_{n,j}}{2} + \frac{S_n}{T} \tag{5.1}$$

The holding cost at each stage, except for the final stage (the end retailers' stage n), is made of two parts: the first one is the carrying cost for the raw materials as they are being converted into finished products during the production portion of the cycle. The second part is the carrying cost of the finished products during the non-production portion of the cycle. During the production time, the average annual inventory of raw material as well as finished products is equal to $\left.\prod_{s=i}^{n} K_s T D_{i,j}^2 \middle/ 2P_{i,j}\right.$

since T_i is equal to $\prod_{s=i}^{n} K_s T$. During the non-production time, the inventory drops for every T_{i+1} years by $T_{i+1}D_{ij}$ starting from $(T_i - T_{i+1})D_{ij}$ as shown in Figure 4.6. Hence, the inventory holding during the non-production part of the cycle is $(T_i - T_{i+1})D_{ij} + (T_i - 2T_{i+1})D_{ij} + \cdots + T_{i+1}D_{ij}$. Since $T_i = K_i T_{i+1}$ this inventory holding can be rewritten as $T_{i+1}(K_i - 1)D_{ij} + T_{i+1}(K_i - 2)D_{ij} + \cdots + T_{i+1}D_{ij}$ which is equal to $\frac{T_{i+1}D_{ij}(K_i - 1)}{2}$. Once again, the inventory holding during the non-production part of the cycle can be rewritten as $\frac{\prod_{s=i+1}^{n} K_s T D_{i,j}}{2}(K_i - 1)$. Therefore, the total annual cost for any firm at any stage, except for the final stage, is represented by

$$TC_{i,j} = \frac{\prod_{s=i}^{n} K_s T D_{i,j}^2 h_{i-1}}{2P_{i,j}} + \frac{\prod_{s=i+1}^{n} K_s T D_{i,j}}{2}(K_i(1 + D_{i,j}/P_{i,j}) - 1)h_i + \frac{S_i}{\prod_{s=i}^{n} K_s T} \tag{5.2}$$

We assume that $K_n = 1$.

The total cost for the entire supply chain is:

$$TC = \sum_{i,j} TC_{i,j} \tag{5.3}$$

We can write TC as:

$$TC = T \left\{ \frac{ADh_n + \sum_{i=1}^{n-1} \sum_j IC_{i,j} A}{2A} \right\} + \frac{1}{T} \sum_{i=1}^{n} \frac{S_i}{\prod_{s=i}^{n} K_s} \tag{5.4}$$

where A is the product of all production rates for all the companies in the supply chain.

and $IC_{i,j} = \dfrac{\prod_{s=i}^{n} K_s TD_{i,j}^2 h_{i-1}}{2P_{i,j}} + \dfrac{\prod_{s=i+1}^{n} K_s TD_{i,j}}{2} (K_i(1 + D_{i,j}/P_{i,j}) - 1)h_i$

We define $\alpha_0 = (h_0 + h_1) \sum_j D_{1,J}^2 B_{1,J} + A \sum_j D_{1,j} h_1$, $\psi_0 = 0$ and $\varphi_1 = S_1$.

For i=1, 2, 3… n-1 and for all j, we define α_i, ψ_i and φ_i as follows:

$$\alpha_i = (h_i + h_{i+1}) \sum_j D_{i+1,j}^2 B_{i+1,J} + A \sum_j D_{i+1,j} h_{i+1} - A \sum_j D_{i,j} h_i \tag{5.5}$$

$$\psi_i = K_{i-1} \psi_{i-1} + \alpha_{i-1} \tag{5.6}$$

$$\varphi_i = \left(S_i + \frac{\varphi_{i-1}}{K_{i-1}} \right) \tag{5.7}$$

For convenience and handiness, we rewrite Eq.(5.4) in the following manner(see the Appendix A):

$$TC = TY + \frac{W}{T} \tag{5.8}$$

where

$$Y = \frac{K_{n-1} \psi_{n-1} + \alpha_{n-1}}{2A} \tag{5.9}$$

$$\text{and} \quad W = \left(S_n + \frac{\varphi_{n-1}}{K_{n-1}} \right) \tag{5.10}$$

Now, the annual total cost for the entire supply chain in Eq. (5.8) can be represented by factorizing the term $1/T$ and completing the perfect square, one has

$$TC = \frac{1}{T}\left(T^2 Y - 2T\sqrt{YW} + W + 2T\sqrt{YW}\right) \tag{5.11}$$

Factorizing the perfect squared trinomial in a squared binomial we obtain:

$$TC = \frac{1}{T}\left(T\sqrt{Y} - \sqrt{W}\right)^2 + 2\sqrt{YW} \tag{5.12}$$

It is worthy pointing out that Eq. (5.12) reaches minimum with respect to T when setting $\left(T\sqrt{Y} - \sqrt{W}\right)^2 = 0$

Hence, the optimal basic cycle time T^* is

$$T^* = \sqrt{\frac{W}{Y}} \tag{5.13}$$

Substituting Eq. (5.13) into Eq. (5.8), the minimum value for the annual total cost for the entire supply chain is:

$$TC = 2\sqrt{YW} \tag{5.14}$$

       The optimal basic cycle time T^* is a function of the integer multipliers $\left(K_{n-1}, K_{n-2}, K_{n-3}, \ldots K_1\right)$. The method of perfect square is used to drive the optimal values of these integer multipliers iteratively, or in a recursive fashion. Substituting from Eq.(5.9) and Eq.(5.10) for Y and W respectively into Eq.(5.14) we get:

$$TC = \sqrt{\frac{2}{A}}\left\{\left(K_{n-1}\psi_{n-1} + \alpha_{n-1}\right)\left(S_n + \frac{\varphi_{n-1}}{K_{n-1}}\right)\right\}^{\frac{1}{2}}$$

$$= \sqrt{\frac{2}{A}}\left\{K_{n-1}\psi_{n-1}S_n + \psi_{n-1}\varphi_{n-1} + \alpha_{n-1}S_n + \alpha_{n-1}\frac{\varphi_{n-1}}{K_{n-1}}\right\}^{\frac{1}{2}}$$

$$= \sqrt{\frac{2}{A}}\left\{K_{n-1}\psi_{n-1}S_n + \psi_{n-1}\varphi_{n-1} + \alpha_{n-1}S_n + \alpha_{n-1}\frac{\varphi_{n-1}}{K_{n-1}}\right\}^{\frac{1}{2}}$$

$$= \sqrt{\frac{2}{A}}\left\{K_{n-1}\psi_{n-1}S_n + \alpha_{n-1}\frac{\varphi_{n-1}}{K_{n-1}} + \psi_{n-1}\varphi_{n-1} + \alpha_{n-1}S_n\right\}^{\frac{1}{2}}$$

$$= \sqrt{\frac{2}{A}} \left\{ \frac{1}{K_{n-1}} \left(K^2_{n-1} \psi_{n-1} S_n - 2K_{n-1} \sqrt{\psi_{n-1} S_n \alpha_{n-1} \varphi_{n-1}} + \alpha_{n-1} \varphi_{n-1} \right) + \psi_{n-1} \varphi_{n-1} + 2K_{n-1} \sqrt{\psi_{n-1} S_n \alpha_{n-1} \varphi_{n-1}} + \alpha_{n-1} S_n \right\}^{\frac{1}{2}}$$

$$\sqrt{\frac{2}{A}} \left\{ \frac{1}{K_{n-1}} \left[K_{n-1} \sqrt{\psi_{n-1} S_n} - \sqrt{\alpha_{n-1} \varphi_{n-1}} \right]^2 + \left[\sqrt{\psi_{n-1} \varphi_{n-1}} + \sqrt{\alpha_{n-1} S_n} \right]^2 \right\}^{\frac{1}{2}} \tag{5.15}$$

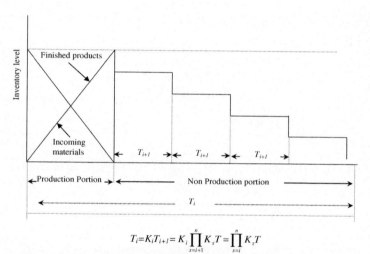

$$T_i = K_i T_{i+1} = K_i \prod_{s=i+1}^{n} K_s T = \prod_{s=i}^{n} K_s T$$

Figure 5.1: Raw materials and finished products at two consecutive stages

From (5.15) setting $\left[K_{n-1}\sqrt{\psi_{n-1}S_n} - \sqrt{\alpha_{n-1}\varphi_{n-1}}\right]^2 = 0$, the optimal value of integer multiplier K_{n-1} is derived as follows:

$$K^*_{n-1} = \sqrt{\frac{\alpha_{n-1}\varphi_{n-1}}{\psi_{n-1}S_n}} \qquad (5.16)$$

Since the value of K_{n-1} is a positive integer, the following condition must be satisfied:

$$(K^*_{n-1}).(K^*_{n-1} - 1) \le (K^*_{n-1})^2 \le K^*_{n-1}.(K^*_{n-1} + 1) \qquad (5.17)$$

To drive the optimal value of integer multiplier K_{n-2}, we can rewrite the term $\sqrt{\psi_{n-1}\varphi_{n-1}}$ in Eq. (5.15) as follows:

$$\sqrt{\psi_{n-1}\varphi_{n-1}} = \left\{\left(K_{n-1}\psi_{n-1} + \alpha_{n-1}\right)\left(S_n + \frac{\varphi_{n-1}}{K_{n-1}}\right)\right\}^{\frac{1}{2}}$$

$$= \left\{\frac{1}{K_{n-2}}\left[K_{n-2}\sqrt{\psi_{n-2}S_{n-1}} - \sqrt{\alpha_{n-2}\varphi_{n-2}}\right]^2 + \left[\sqrt{\psi_{n-2}\varphi_{n-2}} + \sqrt{\alpha_{n-2}S_{n-1}}\right]\right\}^{\frac{1}{2}} \qquad (5.18)$$

From Eq. (5.18), setting $\left[K_{n-2}\sqrt{\psi_{n-2}S_{n-1}} - \sqrt{\alpha_{n-2}\varphi_{n-2}}\right]^2 = 0$, the optimal value of the integer multiplier K_{n-2} is derived as follows:

$$K^*_{n-2} = \sqrt{\frac{\alpha_{n-2}\varphi_{n-2}}{\psi_{n-2}S_{n-1}}} \qquad (5.19)$$

Since the value of K_{n-2} is a positive integer, the following condition must be satisfied:

$$(K^*_{n-2}).(K^*_{n-2} - 1) \le (K^*_{n-2})^2 \le K^*_{n-2}.(K^*_{n-2} + 1) \qquad (5.20)$$

We continue carrying out this iterative process until the optimal value of the integer multiplier K_1 is reached:

$$K^*_1 = \sqrt{\frac{\alpha_1\varphi_1}{\psi_1 S_2}} \qquad (5.21)$$

Substituting $\psi_1 = \alpha_0 = (h_0 + h_1)\sum_j D^2_{1,j}B_{1,J} + A\sum_j D_{1,j}h_1$, $\varphi_1 = S_1$ and

$\alpha_1 = \left(h_1 + h_2\right)\sum_j D_{2,j}^2 B_{2,j} + A\sum_j D_{2,j}h_2 - A\sum_j D_{1,j}h_1$ Into Eq. (5.21) we obtain:

$$K^*_1 = \sqrt{\frac{\left(\left(h_1 + h_2\right)\sum_j D_{2,j}^2 B_{2,j} + A\sum_j D_{2,j}h_2 - A\sum_j D_{1,j}h_1\right)S_1}{\left(\left(h_0 + h_1\right)\sum_j D_{1,j}^2 B_{1,J} + A\sum_j D_{1,j}h_1\right)S_2}} \tag{5.22}$$

Since the value of K_1 is a positive integer, the following condition must be satisfied:

$$(K^*_1).(K^*_1 - 1) \le (K^*_1)^2 \le K^*_1.(K^*_1 + 1) \tag{5.23}$$

After deriving the optimal value of K_1 from Eq. (5.18) and Eq. (5.19), the optimal value of K_2 can be derived as follows:

$$K^*_2 = \sqrt{\frac{\alpha_2 \varphi_2}{\psi_2 S_3}} \tag{5.24}$$

Substituting: $\alpha_2 = \left(h_2 + h_3\right)\sum_j D_{3,j}^2 B_{3,J} + A\sum_j D_{3,j}h_3 - A\sum_j D_{2,j}h_2$, and

$\varphi_2 = \left(S_2 + \dfrac{S_1}{K_1}\right)$, we obtain:

$$K^*_2 = \sqrt{\frac{\left(\left(h_2 + h_3\right)\sum_j D_{3,j}^2 B_{3,J} + A\sum_j D_{3,j}h_3 - A\sum_j D_{2,j}h_2\right)\left(S_2 + S_1/K_1\right)}{\psi_2 S_3}} \tag{5.25}$$

Where:

$$\psi_2 = K_1\left[\left(h_0 + h_1\right)\sum_j D_{1,j}^2 B_{1,J} + A\sum_j D_{1,j}h_1\right] +$$

$$\left[\left(h_1 + h_2\right)\sum_j D_{2,j}^2 B_{i,J} + A\sum_j D_{2,j}h_2 - A\sum_j D_{1,j}h_1\right]$$

Since the value of K_2 is a positive integer, the following condition must be satisfied:

$$(K^*_2).(K^*_2 - 1) \le (K^*_2)^2 \le K^*_2.(K^*_2 + 1) \tag{5.26}$$

We follow this recursive procedure each time driving the optimal K_{i+1} from the previously derived optimal K_i. When the optimal K_{n-1} is derived, then optimal basic cycle time T^*, which is a function of the integer multipliers $\left(K_{n-1}, K_{n-2}, K_{n-3}, \dots K_1\right)$, can be derived from Eq. (5.24).

5.3 Solution Procedure

Based on the recursive structures developed above, the following solution procedure is proposed:

Step 0: Set: $\psi_0 = 0$, $\alpha_0 = (h_0 + h_1)\sum_j D_{1,j}^2 B_{1,J} + A\sum_j D_{1,j}h_1$, $K_0 = 0$, $\varphi_1 = S_1$

Step 1: for i=1,2,3,...,n-1 and for all j compute :

$$\alpha_i = (h_i + h_{i+1})\sum_j D_{i+1,j}^2 B_{i+1,j} + A\sum_j D_{i+1,j}h_{i+1} - A\sum_j D_{i,j}h_i$$

$$\psi_i = K_{i-1}\psi_{i-1} + \alpha_{i-1}$$

$$\varphi_i = \left(S_i + \frac{\varphi_{i-1}}{K_{i-1}}\right)$$

$$K_i^* = \sqrt{\frac{\alpha_i\varphi_i}{\psi_i S_{i+1}}} \text{ , s.t. } (K_i^*).(K_i^* - 1) \le (K_i^*)^2 \le (K_i^*).(K_i^* + 1)$$

Step 2: Use Eq. (5.6) to compute Y and use Eq. (5.7) to compute W.

Step 3: Compute $T^* = \sqrt{W/Y}$

5.4 Numerical Example

The purpose of this subsection is to illustrate the application of the developed algebraic solution procedure by a numerical example. This example represents a four-stage supply chain consisting of one supplier, two manufacturers, four distributors, and six retailers. The relevant data is shown in Table 4.6. It is also assumed that holding cost for the supplier's supplier is $h_0=0.1$.

In addition, it is also assumed that manufacturer 1 supplies distributors 1 and 2; manufacturer 2 supplies distributors 3 and 4; distributor 1 supplies retailers 1 and 2; distributor 2 supplies retailer 3; distributor 3 supplies retailer 4; distributor 4 supplies retailers 5 and 6.

By applying the above solution procedure, the results of the proposed example model are presented in Table 4.7. We use the data of this example to analyze the effect of the setup and holding costs on the integer multipliers; and system's total cost. This sensitivity analysis is presented in Tables 4.8-4.11. From this simple sensitivity analysis we can conclude that if the suppliers increase their setup cost, then their integer multipliers tend to increase. This also tends to happen if the manufacturers decrease their setup cost. If the distributors decrease their holding costs or the retailers increase their holding costs, then integer multipliers for the distributors tend to increase.

Table 4.4: Data for the numerical example

Stage i	Firm index j	Parent(i,j)	Holding cost Incoming hi	Annual demand Dij	Setup cost Si
Suppliers	1	_	0.8	130000	1000
Manufactures	1	1	2	60000	200
	2	1	2	70000	200
Distributors	1	1	4	35000	50
	2	1	4	25000	50
	3	2	4	30000	50
	4	2	4	40000	50
Retailers	1	1	7	20000	10
	2	1	7	15000	10
	3	2	7	25000	10
	4	3	7	30000	10
	5	4	7	15000	10
	6	4	7	25000	10

Table 4.5: Results for the numerical example

	Solution
Suppliers' integer multiplier	2
Manufactures' integer multiplier	2
Distributors' integer multiplier	2
Retailers' basic cycle time	0.0134
Supply chain total cost	5,3872.485

Table 4.6: Sensitivity analysis when the suppliers' setup cost changes

S_1	800	900	1100	1200
Suppliers' integer multiplier	2	2	2	3
Manufactures' integer multiplier	2	2	2	2
Distributors' integer multiplier	2	2	2	1
Retailers' basic cycle time	0.0129	0.0131	0.0136	0.0228
Supply chain total cost	48143.7578	49104.8059	50972.5715	53445.7067

Table 4.7: Sensitivity analysis when the manufactures' setup cost changes

S_2	150	160	210	240
Suppliers' integer multiplier	3	3	2	2
Manufactures' integer multiplier	1	1	2	2
Distributors' integer multiplier	2	2	2	2
Retailers' basic cycle time	0.0172	0.0174	0.0136	0.0138
Supply chain total cost	49746.75	50326.35	50788.89	51519.70

Table 4.8: Sensitivity analysis when the distributors' holding cost changes

h_3	3.2	3.6	4.4	4.8
Suppliers' integer multiplier	2	2	2	2
Manufactures' integer multiplier	2	2	2	2
Distributors' integer multiplier	2	2	2	1
Retailers' basic cycle time	0.0137	0.0136	0.0132	0.0250
Supply chain total cost	48802.54	49428.89	50658.36	52700.44

Table 4.9: Sensitivity analysis when the retailers' holding cost changes

h_4	5.6	6.3	7.7	8.4
Suppliers' integer multiplier	2	2	2	2
Manufactures' integer multiplier	2	2	2	2
Distributors' integer multiplier	1	1	2	2
Retailers' basic cycle time	0.0265	0.0259	0.0132	0.0131
Supply chain total cost	49844.9424	51035.6570	50652.8627	51251.17

5.5 Summary

In this chapter, a generalized algebraic optimization method for the integer multiplier inventory coordination mechanism is developed. The developed method easily establishes the convexity of the cost function.

Chapter 6

The Integrated Production Inventory Transportation Model

6.1 Introduction

The benefits of inventory coordination and information sharing among the supply chain participants, have received significant attention in the literature. Research findings in this area revealed that information sharing and coordinated inventory replenishments can help reduce the inventory and order costs as well as transportation costs. Collaborative transportation management in supply chain can significantly reduce the retailer's total costs and improve the retailer's service level (Chan and Zhang, 2011). In this chapter, the modeling approach developed in chapter 4 and chapter 5 is applied the integrated supply chain inventory transportation model.

6.2 The Single-Manufacturer Multi-Buyer Integrated Inventory Supply Chain

In this section, we use the model presented in Hoque(2008) to look into how The algebraic approach can be used to provide easier and faster solutions. The next subsections present the problem definition, assumptions, notations, the detailed development of the models.

Notations and assumptions

As in Hoque(2008), the following notations are used in developing the model:

D =The total demand rate in the supply chain per year;

P_i=Production rate at the vendor;

h_i =Inventory holding cost per item per year for the vendor;

S=Vendor's production set up cost per lot;

Z=the size of batch transferred from the vendor to the buyers;

n= the number of equal sized batches in a lot;

D_i=The annual demand rate the ith buyer;

h_i =Inventory holding cost per item per year for the ith buyer;

S_i =Order cost the ith buyer per order.

Assumptions for the single-vendor multi-buyers supply chain model:

    (a) A single product is produced by the vendor and transferred to the buyers;

    (b) Replenishment is instantaneous;

    (c) Production rates and Demand rate are deterministic and uniform;

    (d) A lot produced by the vendor and sent in equal batches to the buyers;

    (e) Complete information sharing policy is adopted;

    (f) There is no backlogging.

6.3 The Development of the Model:

The total cost for the vendor consists of the inventory carrying cost and production set-up cost. In each production cycle, the vendor produces a lot of size nZ. Each batch of size Z is transferred to the buyers as soon as its processing is finished, so the total cost for the vendor per year is

$$TC_v = \frac{Dh\,Z}{2P} + \frac{DS}{nZ} \tag{6.1}$$

Hoque(2008) has shown that the average annual total cost of inventory, transportation and ordering for the ith buyer is given by

$$TC_{Bi} = \frac{D_i Z h_i}{2D} + \frac{(n-1)}{2}\left(\frac{1}{D} - \frac{1}{P}\right)D_i h_i Z + D\left(S_i + nT_i\right)/nZ \tag{6.2}$$

Hence the total annual cost for the integrated vendor-buyers supply chain is

$$TC = \frac{Z}{2}\left[\frac{Dh}{P} + \left\{\frac{1}{D} + (n-1)\left(\frac{1}{D} - \frac{1}{P}\right)\right\}\sum_{i=1}^{m} D_i h_i\right] + \frac{1}{Z}\left[D\left\{\frac{S + \sum_{i=1}^{m} S_i}{n} + \sum_{i=1}^{m} T_i\right\}\right] \tag{6.3}$$

Equation (6.3) can be rewritten as

$$TC = ZY + \frac{W}{Z} \tag{6.4}$$

Where

$$Y = \frac{\left[\dfrac{Dh}{P} + \left\{ \dfrac{1}{D} + (n-1)\left(\dfrac{1}{D} - \dfrac{1}{P} \right) \right\} \sum_{i=1}^{m} D_i h_i \right]}{2} \qquad (6.5)$$

And

$$W = \left[D \left\{ \frac{S + \sum_{i=1}^{m} S_i}{n} + \sum_{i=1}^{m} T_i \right\} \right] \qquad (6.6)$$

Now applying the algebraic procedure proposed by Cárdenas-Barrón (2007), the annual total cost for the entire supply chain in Eq. (6.4) can be represented by factorizing the term $1/Z$ and completing the perfect square, one has

$$TC = \frac{1}{Z} \left(Z^2 Y - 2Z\sqrt{YW} + W + 2Z\sqrt{YW} \right)^2 \qquad (6.7)$$

Factorizing the perfect squared trinomial in a squared binomial we obtain:

$$TC = \frac{1}{Z} \left(Z\sqrt{Y} - \sqrt{W} \right)^2 + 2\sqrt{YW} \qquad (6.8)$$

It is worthy pointing out that Eq. (6.8) reaches minimum with respect to Z when setting

$$\left(Z\sqrt{Y} - \sqrt{W} \right)^2 = 0$$

Hence, the optimal batch size Z^* is

$$Z^* = \sqrt{\frac{W}{Y}} \qquad (6.9)$$

Now for the entire supply chain, the minimum annual total cost is given as

$$TC = 2\sqrt{YW} \qquad (6.10)$$

The optimal batch size Z^* is a function of the integer multiplier n . We use the method of perfect square to drive the optimal value of this integer multiplier. Substituting for Y and W into Eq.(6.10) we get

$$TC = \sqrt{2}\left\{(na+b)\left(c+\frac{d}{n}\right)\right\}^{\frac{1}{2}}$$ (6.11)

Where

$$a = \left(\frac{1}{D} - \frac{1}{P}\right)\sum_{i=1}^{m} D_i h_i$$

$$b = \frac{Dh}{P} + \frac{1}{P}\sum_{i=1}^{m} D_i h_i$$

$$c = D\sum_{i=1}^{m} T_i$$

$$d = D\left(S + \sum_{i=1}^{m} S_i\right)$$

Rewriting Eq.(6.11)

$$\sqrt{2}\left\{\frac{1}{n}\left[n\sqrt{ac} - \sqrt{bd}\right]^2 + \left[\sqrt{ad} + \sqrt{bc}\right]^2\right\}^{\frac{1}{2}}$$ (6.12)

From (6.12) setting

$$\left[n\sqrt{ac} - \sqrt{bd}\right]^2 = 0,$$

the optimal value of the integer multiplier n is derived as follows:

$$n^* = \sqrt{\frac{bd}{ac}}$$ (6.13)

Since the value of n* is a positive integer, the following condition must be satisfied

$$(n^*).(n^* - 1) \leq \left(\frac{bd}{ac}\right) \leq n^*.(n^* + 1)$$ (6.14)

Now, we can substitute n* from Eq.(6.13) into Eq.(6.9) to find the optimal batch size Z*. Also, substituting n* from Eq.(6.13) into Eq.(6.12) derives the optimal annual total cost in the following closed form

$$TC^* = \sqrt{2}\left[\sqrt{ad} + \sqrt{bc}\right]$$ (6.15)

If we substitute for a, b, c and d into Eq.(6.15), we get

$$TC^* = \sqrt{2}\left[\sqrt{D\left(\frac{1}{D}-\frac{1}{P}\right)\left(S+\sum_{i=1}^{m}S_i\right)\sum_{i=1}^{m}D_ih_i} + \sqrt{D\left(\frac{Dh}{P}+\frac{1}{P}\sum_{i=1}^{m}D_ih_i\right)\sum_{i=1}^{m}T_i}\right]$$ (6.16)

Eq.(6.16) represents the minimum annual total cost for the integrated supply chain system expressed only in terms of the production rate, demand rate and cost parameters.

6.4 Integrating the Transportation Costs into the Model

If we consider the transportation cost as a function of the batch size, then expected total cost per unit time in Eq.(6.8) should be expressed as:

$$TC = \frac{1}{Z}\left(Z\sqrt{Y}-\sqrt{W}\right)^2 + 2\sqrt{YW} + F(n,Z)$$

$$TC = \frac{1}{Z}\left(Z\sqrt{Y}-\sqrt{W}\right)^2 + 2\sqrt{YW} + \sum_{i=1}^{m}F(n,z_i)$$ (6.17)

The quantity discount transportation cost structure followed in the development of the model is defined as:

$$F(n,Z) = \begin{cases} c_0D & Z\in[0,M_1] \\ c_1D & Z\in[M_1,M_2] \\ c_2D & Z\in[M_2,M_3] \\ ..... & .... \\ c_mD & Z\in[M_m,\infty] \end{cases}$$

Where $c_m \prec ... \prec c_1 \prec c_0$ are the different unit transportation costs as in Ertogral et al.(2007).

6.5 Numerical Example

To demonstrate this model, we consider the example with the data in Table 1. In addition to this data, the following cost parameters are assumed for the vendor: S=400, h=0.15, P=1800. The quantity discount structure for this example is shown in Table 2.

Table 1. Data for the example

Buyer i	Si	Di	hi	Ti
1	10	250	0.50	18
2	12	200	0.40	22
3	13	180	0.45	24
4	20	150	0.60	26
5	25	210	0.30	16

Table 2. Quantity discount structure

Range	Unit shipping cost
$Q < 100$	0.35
$100 \leq Q < 150$	0.3
$150 \leq Q < 200$	0.25
$200 \leq Q < 250$	0.20
$250 \leq Q < 500$	0.15
$500 \leq Q < 1000$	0.10
$1000 \leq Q$	0.8

The solution for this example obtained by applying the developed solution procedure provides an optimal batch size of 2263.695 for the vendor. The optimal number of shipments is given as 3. The detailed are represented in Table 3. Table 4 shows the cost savings for the buyers under collaborative transportation.

Table 3. The solution for the numerical example

Cost Component	Under Non-CT	Under CT
Lot size, batch sizes and its no.	2263.695, 754.56, 3	
Set up cost of the manufacturer	174.94	174.94
Inventory cost of the manufacturer	31.13	31.13
Ordering costs of buyers	34.99	34.99
Inventory costs of the buyers	317.87	317.87
Domestic Transportation cost	136.26	136.26
Int' transportation cost	264.00	99.00
Total cost of the manufacturer	206.06	206.06
Total cost of the buyers	489.12	640.03
Total cost	959.18	794.18

Table 4. The Cost Savings for the buyers

Buyer	Zi	Transportation Under Non-CT		Transportation Under CT		Saving	Saving %
		PU	PUT	PU	PUT		
1	190.55	0.25	62.50	0.10	25.00	37.50	60.00
2	152.44	0.25	50.00	0.10	20.00	30.00	60.00
3	137.19	0.30	54.00	0.10	18.00	36.00	66.67
4	114.33	0.30	45.00	0.10	15.00	30.00	66.67
5	160.06	0.25	52.50	0.10	21.00	31.50	60.00
Total	754.56	Average:(0.27)	264		99.00	165	

Chapter 7

A Multi-Stage Supply Chain Model with Stochastic Demands

7.1 Introduction

In this chapter, a stochastic four-stage supply chain model is presented. The model is formulated for three inventory coordination mechanism. In section 7.1 the problem is defined. In section 7.2 the assumptions are stated and the notations are declared. Section 7.3 presents the development of the model under the equal cycle coordination mechanism. Section 7.4 presents the development of the model under the integer multiplier coordination mechanism. The power of two coordination mechanism formulation is presented in section 7.5. In section 5.6 the decentralized policy is presented. Section 7.7 describes a coordination benefits sharing scheme. Numerical analysis for illustrative purposes is presented in section 7.8.

7.2 Problem Definition

In recent years, supply chain production and inventory coordination received a lot of attention. Most of the developed models deal with two-stage chains. Even when multi-stage supply chains are considered, most of the developed models are based on the restrictive assumption of deterministic demand. Therefore, there is a need to analyze models that relax the usual assumptions to allow for a more realistic analysis of the supply chain. In this part of the research, we consider the case of a four-stage supply chain where a firm can supply many customers with a single product. This supply chain system involves suppliers, manufactures, distributors and retailers. Production and inventory decisions are made at the suppliers and manufactures levels. The production rates for the suppliers and manufactures are assumed finite. In addition the demand from each retailer is assumed to be stochastic. Unsatisfied demands at the end retailers are backordered. The problem is to coordinate production and inventory decisions across the supply chain so that the total cost of the system is minimized, while satisfying the service level constraints. The service level is defined as the proportion of demands that should be met at the end retailers.

7.3   Assumptions and Notations:

In addition to the notations stated in the previous chapter, the following notations are needed for the models developed in this chapter:

x = A random variable describing the demand at retailer j.

$f_{4,j}(x,T)$ = The continuous probability density of the customer demand received at retailer j in stage four for the period T.

π = The shortage penalty per unit short

In developing the models, the following assumptions are made:

- A single product is produced and distributed through a four stage, multi customer, non-serial , supply chain

- Demand rates are stochastic

- Unsatisfied demands at the end retailers are backordered

- Ordering /setup costs are the same for firms at the same stage

- Holding costs cost are the same for firms at the same stage

- Shortage costs are the same for firms at the same stage

- A lot produced at stage is sent in equal shipments to the downstream stage.

7.4   Equal cycle time coordination mechanism

Let i=1,2, and 4 denote the stage index in the supply chain. And let j =1,2,…, J_i be an index denoting firms within each stage. Referring to Figure 7.1, two cases exist at an end retailer: case A and Case B. Case A occurs if $x \leq TD_{4,j}$ and no shortage is faced by the retailer in this case. The holding cost per unit time is $h_4 T \dfrac{(TD_{4,j} - x)}{T} + h_4 \dfrac{Tx}{2T}$ which is equal to $h_4 \left(TD_{4,j} - \dfrac{x}{2} \right)$.

Case B occurs if x>TD$_{4,j}$ and shortage is faced by the retailer in this case. The holding cost per unit time in this case is $h_4 \dfrac{TD_{4,j}.T_1}{2T}$ which is equal to $h_4 \dfrac{(TD_{4,j})^2}{2x}$.

The shortage cost per unit time is $\pi_4 \dfrac{(x - TD_{4,j}).T_2}{2T}$ which is equal to $\pi_4 \dfrac{(x - TD_{4,j})^2}{2x}$.

Now the expected total cost per unit time for a downstream retailer can be formulated as:

$$TC_{4,j} = h_4 \int_0^{TD_{4,j}} \left(TD_{4,j} - \frac{x}{2} \right) f_{4,j}(x,T) dx + h_4 \int_{TD_{4,j}}^{\infty} \frac{(TD)^2}{2x} f_{4,j}(x,T) dx$$
$$+ \pi \int_{TD}^{\infty} \frac{1}{2x} (x - TD)^2 f_{4,j}(x,T) dx + \frac{A_4}{T} \tag{7.1}$$

The first and second terms in Equation (7.1) represents the average carrying cost at an end retailer, while the third term is the average shortage cost. The last term is the replenishment cost, which occurs in every period of length T when the product is ordered.

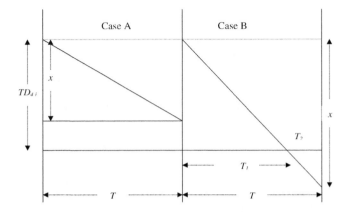

Figure 7.1: Inventory level at a retailer

The expected total cost per unit time for a distributor at stage three is:

$$TC_{3,j} = \frac{TD_{3,j}h_3}{2} + \frac{A_3}{T} \tag{7.2}$$

The annual total cost for a manufacturer at the second stage is made up of two parts: the first is cost of carrying raw material as they are transformed to final products; and the second is the cost of holding finished goods. This occurs only during the production portion of the cycle. During the non-production portion of the equal cycle the inventory drops to zero because the whole amount produced is immediately shipped to the retailer stage. During the production portion, the average raw material and finished products inventory is $TD_{2,j}/2$. Since the production rate is $P_{2,j}$, the per unit time average raw material and finished goods holding costs are $h_1TD^2{}_{2,j}/2P_{2,j}$ and $h_2TD^2{}_{2,j}/2P_{2,j}$, see Khouja(2003). Hence the expected total cost for a firm at stage 2 (i.e. manufacturer) is:

$$TC_{2,j} = \frac{TD_{2,j}^2}{2P_{2,j}}(h_1 + h_2) + \frac{A_2}{T} \tag{7.3}$$

Similarly the expected total cost for a firm at stage 1 (i.e. supplier) is:

$$TC_{1,j} = \frac{TD_{1,j}^2}{2P_{1,j}}(h_0 + h_1) + \frac{A_1}{T} \tag{7.4}$$

Now the expected total per unit time cost for the entire supply chain is:

$$TC = \sum_{ij} TC_{ij} \tag{7.5}$$

7.5   Integer Multipliers Coordination Mechanism

For the integer multipliers coordination mechanism, firms at the same stage of the supply chain use the same cycle time. And the cycle time at each stage is an integer multiplier of the cycle time used at the adjacent downstream stage. In this case, the cycle time of a retailer is T and that of a distributor is K_3T. A manufacturer will have a cycle time of K_2K_3T. The cycle time of a supplier is a multiple of that of the manufacturer and is equal to $K_1K_2 K_3T$. Where K_1, K_2, and K_3 are positive integers.

Since all retailers follow a basic replenishment cycle of length T, the total cost per unit time for retailer j is given by the same expression (7.1) in the previous section. The total cost for a firm at stage 3 (i.e. distributor) is given by:

$$TC_{3,j} = \frac{(K_3 - 1)h_3 TD_{3,j}}{2} + \frac{A_3}{K_3T} \tag{7.6}$$

The total cost for a firm at stage 2 (i.e. manufacturer) is given by:

$$TC_{2,j} = \frac{K_2 K_3 TD_{2,j}^2 h_1}{2P_{2,j}} + \frac{K_3 TD_{2,j}}{2}(K_2(1 + D_{2,j}/P_{2,j}) - 1)h_2 + \frac{A_2}{K_2 K_3 T} \tag{7.7}$$

The cost of carrying raw material as it is being converted into finished goods is given by the first term on the right-hand side of Eq. (7.7) .However, the second term is made up of two parts. The first part is $K_2 TD^2{}_{2,j} h_2 / 2 P_{2,j}$ which is the per unit time holding cost of the finished goods for the non-production portion of the cycle and similar to the cost in the equal cycle mechanism. The second part is $TD_{2,j}(k_2 - 1)h_2 / 2$ which represents the per unit time holding cost for the non-production portion of the cycle, see Khouja. (2003).

Similarly the total cost for a firm at stage 1 (i.e. supplier) is:

$$TC_{1,j} = \frac{K_1 K_2 K_3 TD_{1,j}^2 h_0}{2P_{1,j}} + \frac{K_2 K_3 TD}{2}(K_1(1 + D_{1,j}/P_{1,j}) - 1)h_1 + \frac{A_1}{K_1 K_2 K_3 T}$$

$$(5.8)$$

7.6 Powers of Two Multipliers Coordination Mechanism

For the integer powers of two multipliers, also two cases exist at an end retailer: case A and Case B.

Case A occurs if $x \le 2^{K_{4,j}} TD_{4,j}$ and no shortage is faced by the retailer in this case. The holding cost per unit time is $h_4 T \dfrac{\left(2^{K_{4,j}} TD_{4,j} - x\right)}{T} + h_4 \dfrac{Tx}{2T}$ which is equal to

$$h_4 \left(2^{K_{4,j}} TD_{4,j} - \frac{x}{2}\right).$$

Case B occurs if $x \succ 2^{K_{4,j}} TD_{4,j}$ and shortage is faced by the retailer in this case. The holding cost per unit time in this case is $h_4 \dfrac{2^{K_{4,j}} TD_{4,j}.T_1}{2T}$ which is equal

to $h_4 \dfrac{\left(2^{K_{4,j}} TD_{4,j}\right)^2}{2x}$. The shortage cost per unit time is $\pi_4 \dfrac{(x - 2^{K_{4,j}} TD_{4,j}).T_2}{2T}$ which is

equal to $\pi_4 \dfrac{\left(x - 2^{K_{4,j}} TD_{4,j}\right)^2}{2x}$.

Now the total cost per unit time for the downstream retailer is:

$$TC_{4,j} = h_4 \int_0^{2^{k_4}TD_{4,j}} \left(2^{K_{4,j}} TD_{4,j} - \frac{x}{2} \right) f_{4,j}(x, 2^{K_{4,j}} T) dx +$$

$$h_4 \int_{2^{K_{4,j}}TD_{4,j}}^{\infty} \frac{\left(2^{K_{4,j}} TD \right)^2}{2x} f_{4,j}(x, 2^{K_{4,j}} T) dx$$

$$+ \pi \int_{2^{K_{4,j}}TD}^{\infty} \frac{1}{2x} \left(x - 2^{K_{4,j}} TD \right)^2 f_{4,j}(x, 2^{K_{4,j}} T) dx + \frac{A_4}{2^{K_{4,j}} T} \tag{7.9}$$

The total cost per unit time for the distributor is:

$$TC_3 = \frac{A_3}{2^{K_4} T} + h_3 TD \left(2^{K_3} - 2^{K_4} - \frac{2^{2K_4}}{2^{K_3}} \sum_{v=1}^{m} v \right) \tag{7.10}$$

where m is $\left(2^{K_3} \big/ 2^{K_4} - 1 \right)$,

The first term on the right-hand side of Eq.(7.10) is per unit time order cost. The second term represents the per unit time inventory holding cost of the finished goods received from the manufacturer.

According to Khouja (2003) the total cost per unit time for the manufacturer is:

$$TC_2 = \frac{A_2}{2^{K_2} T} + \frac{2^{K_2} TD^2}{2P_2} (h_1 + h_2) + h_2 TD \left(2^{K_2} - 2^{K_3} - \frac{2^{2K_3}}{2^{K_2}} \sum_{v=1}^{n} v \right) \tag{7.11}$$

where n is $\left(2^{K_2} \big/ 2^{K_3} - 1 \right)$

The first term on the right-hand side of Eq.(7.11) is the per unit time setup cost. The second term represents the per unit time inventory holding cost of the material received from the supplier and the finished goods at the manufacturer during the production cycle. The third term is the per unit time inventory holding cost of the finished goods during the non-production cycle.

Similarly the total cost per unit time for the supplier is

$$TC_1 = \frac{A_1}{2^{K_1} T} + \frac{2^{K_1} TD^2}{2P_1} (h_0 + h_1) + h_1 TD \left(2^{K_1} - 2^{K_2} - \frac{2^{2K_2}}{2^{K1}} \sum_{v=1}^{l} v \right) \tag{7.12}$$

where l is $\left(2^{K_1} \big/ 2^{K_2} - 1 \right)$, see Khouja. (2003).

7.7 The Decentralized Inventory Replenishment Policy

In the previous sections, inventory models were developed under three centralized coordination mechanisms. In this section, we consider the case where each stage optimizes its on decisions in a decentralized fashion. We assume that the partners at the same stage share a common synchronized replenishment cycle time. First the retailers' stage will determine its optimal replenishment cycle time and then the distributors' stage will determine its optimal replenishment cycle, which is assumed to be an integer multiple of the predetermined cycle time at the retailers stage. Similarly, the manufactures will determine their optimal replenishment cycle as an integer multiple of the distributors' replenishment cycle time. And finally the suppliers will determine their optimal replenishment cycle as an integer multiple of the manufactures predetermined replenishment cycle.

The Retailers' Independent Optimization

From Eq.(5.1) the expected total cost at an end retailer is:

$$TC_{4,j} = h_4 \int_0^{TD_{4,j}} \left(TD_{4,j} - \frac{x}{2} \right) f_{4,j}(x,T)dx + h_4 \int_{TD_{4,j}}^{\infty} \frac{(TD)^2}{2x} f_{4,j}(x,T)dx$$

$$+ \pi \int_{TD}^{\infty} \frac{1}{2x}(x - TD)^2 f_{4,j}(x,T)dx + \frac{A_4}{T} \tag{7.13}$$

The expected total cost at the retailers' stage is

$$TC_4 = \sum_{j=1}^{J_4} TC_{4,j} \tag{7.14}$$

The optimal cycle time for the retailers' stage T^*_4 is obtained by minimizing (7.14) using a local search method.

The Distributors' Independent Optimization:

Since the distributors decisions are governed by the retailers' decisions, they must have complete knowledge of the retailers' information, and the distributors' cycle will be set at:

$$T_3 = K_3 T^*_4 \tag{7.15}$$

The total cost for the jth distributor is

$$TC_{3j} = \frac{K_3 T_4^* D_{3,j}^2 h_2}{2P_{3,j}} + \frac{T_4^* D_{3,j}}{2}(K_3(1+D_{3,j}/P_{3,j})-1)h_3 + \frac{A_3}{K_3 T_4^*} \qquad (7.16)$$

The total cost at the distributors' stage is

$$TC_3 = \sum_{j=1}^{6} TC_{3,j} =$$

$$\sum_{j=1}^{J_3}\left(\frac{K_3 T_4^* D_{3,j}^2 h_2}{2P_{3,j}} + \frac{T_4^* D_{3,j}}{2}(K_3(1+D_{3,j}/P_{3,j})-1)h_3 + \frac{A_3}{K_3 T_4^*} \right) =$$

$$K_3 \sum_{j=1}^{J_3}\left(\frac{T_4^* D_{3,j}^2 h_2}{2P_{3,j}} + \frac{T_4^* D_{3,j}}{2}(1+D_{3,j}/P_{3,j})h_3 \right) + \frac{J_3 A_3}{K_3 T_4^*} - \sum_{j=1}^{J_3}\frac{T_4^* D_{3,j}}{2}h_3 \qquad (7.17)$$

Now we can use the method developed in section 4.4 of chapter 4 to obtain the optimal value of K_3. First we rewrite (7.17) in the following manner:

$$TC_3 = K_3 Y + \frac{W}{K_3} - Z \qquad (7.18)$$

Where

$$Y = \sum_{j=1}^{J_3}\left(\frac{T_4^* D_{3,j}^2 h_2}{2P_{3,j}} + \frac{T_4^* D_{3,j}}{2}(1+D_{3,j}/P_{3,j})h_3 \right) \qquad (7.19)$$

$$W = \frac{J_3 A_3}{T_4^*} \qquad (7.20)$$

$$Z = \sum_{j=1}^{J_3}\frac{T_4^* D_{3,j}}{2}h_3 \qquad (7.21)$$

Now, (5.18) can be represented by factorizing the term $1/K_3$ and completing the perfect square, one has:

$$TC_3 = \frac{1}{K_3}\left(K^2Y - 2K_3\sqrt{YW} + W + 2K_3\sqrt{YW}\right) - Z$$

$$= \frac{1}{K_3}\left(K_3\sqrt{Y} - \sqrt{W}\right)^2 + 2\sqrt{YW} - Z \qquad (7.22)$$

It is worthy pointing out that (7.22) reaches minimum with respect to K_3 when setting $\left(K_3\sqrt{Y} - \sqrt{W}\right)^2 = 0$ because the term $2\sqrt{YW} - Z$ is independent of K_3.

Hence, the optimal value of the integer K_3 is

$$K_3^* = \sqrt{\frac{W}{Y}} \qquad (7.23)$$

Substituting from Eq.(7.19) and Eq.(7.20) for Y and W respectively into Eq.(5.23) we get:

$$K_3^* = \sqrt{\frac{J_3 A_3}{T_4^*} \bigg/ \sum_{j=1}^{J_3}\left(\frac{T_4^* D_{3,j}^2 h_2}{2P_{3,j}} + \frac{T_4^* D_{3,j}}{2}(1 + D_{3,j}/P_{3,j})h_3\right)} \qquad (7.24)$$

The Manufacturers' Independent Optimization:

The manufacturers have complete knowledge of the retailers and distributors, and hence they will set their cycle time at:

$$T_2 = K_2 K_3^* T_4^*$$

The manufacturers only need to determine the optimal value of the integer K_2.

The cost for a manufacturer is given by:

$$TC_{2,j} = \frac{K_2 K_3^* T_4^* D_{2,j}^2 h_1}{2P_{2,j}} + \frac{K_3^* T_4^* D_{2,j}}{2}(K_2(1 + D_{2,j}/P_{2,j}) - 1)h_2 + \frac{A_2}{K_2 K_3^* T_4^*} \qquad (7.25)$$

The total cost for firms at stage 2 (i.e. manufacturers) is given by:

$$TC_2 = \sum_{j=1}^{J_2} TC_{2,j} =$$

$$K_2 \sum_{j=1}^{J_2}\left(\frac{K_3^* T_4^* D_{2,j}^2 h_1}{2P_{2,j}} + \frac{K_3^* T_4^* D_{2,j}}{2}(1 + D_{2,j}/P_{2,j})h_2\right) + \frac{J_2 A_2}{K_2 K_3^* T_4^*}$$

$$-\sum_{j=1}^{J_2} \frac{K_3^* T_4^* D_{2,j}}{2} h_2 \tag{7.26}$$

Now if we follow the same method of the previous subsection, the optimal value for the integer multiplier K_2 is

$$K_2^* = \sqrt{\frac{(J_2 A_2)/(K_3^* T_4^*)}{\sum_{j=1}^{J_2} \left(\frac{K_3^* T_4^* D_{2,j}^2 h_1}{2 P_{2,j}} + \frac{K_3^* T_4^* D_{2,j}}{2} (1 + D_{2,j}/P_{2,j}) h_2 \right)}} \tag{7.27}$$

The Suppliers Independent Optimization:

The suppliers' decisions are governed by the decisions at the downstream stages. They will set their synchronized cycle time at:

$$T_1 = K_1 K_2^* K_3^* T_4^*$$

The total cost at the suppliers' stage is

$$TC_1 = K_1 \sum_{j=1}^{J_1} \left(\frac{K_2^* K_3^* T_4^* D_{1,j}^2 h_0}{2 P_{1,j}} + \frac{K_2^* K_3^* T_4^* D_{1,j}}{2} (1 + D_{1,j}/P_{1,j}) h_1 \right) + \frac{J_1 A_1}{K_1 K_2^* K_3^* T_4^*}$$

$$-\sum_{j=1}^{J_1} \frac{K_2^* K_3^* T_4^* D_{1,j}^2}{2} h_1 \tag{7.28}$$

The optimal value for the integer multiplier K_1 is

$$K_1^* = \sqrt{\frac{(J_1 A_1)/(K_2^* K_3^* T_4^*)}{\sum_{j=1}^{J_1} \left(\frac{K_2^* K_3^* T_4^* D_{1,j}^2 h_0}{2 P_{1,j}} + \frac{K_2^* K_3^* T_4^* D_{1,j}}{2} (1 + D_{1,j}/P_{1,j}) h_1 \right)}} \tag{7.29}$$

7.8   Inventory Coordination Benefits Sharing Scheme

In this section we propose a scheme that can be used to share   the savings resulting from implementing any of the investigated inventory coordination mechanisms, among the members of the supply chain in such a way to motivate their implementation.

Since the whole supply chain is driven by the demand at the downstream retailers, the retailers' stage optimum cycle time is considered basic for all upstream stages. In order to entice all stages to adopt the centralized coordination, we first need to ascertain the individual consequences of adopting the joined coordination instead of following the cycle time determined by the retailers. For this purpose we define $ECTC_k(T^*_4 \rightarrow T^*)$ as the economic cost consequence of accepting the centralized replenishment and production decision policy at stage k instead of the decentralized policy. This basically represents the difference between the cost of adopting the joined basic cycle time and its integer multipliers with full coordination (centralized policy), and the cost of using the multiple of the cycle time favored by the retailers' stage (decentralized policy). It is acknowledged that an optimal inventory replenishment policy for a downstream stage is generally sub-optimal for an upstream stage, while an optimal inventory replenishment policy for an upstream stage is generally unacceptable to the downstream stages (Chen and Chen, 2005). In order to induce all parties to adopt a common coordination mechanism, a saving–sharing mechanism should be provided to offset the additional costs that may be incurred by any party due to adopting the joined policy, and then divide the sharing benefits among all supply members. Figure 7.2 shows the proposed savings –sharing scheme. Implementing this procedure will provide a scheme that will allow all supply chain partners to share the coordination benefits.

Step 1:

  Compute: T_4^*, $TC_4(T_4^*)$

Step 2:

  For i=3 to 1

  Compute: K_i, $TC_i(T_4^*, K_i^*)$.

Step 3:

  Compute : $TC(T_4^*) = \sum_{i=1}^{4} TC(T_i^*, K_i^*)$

  Compute : $T^*, K_1^*, K_2^*, K_3^*, TC(T^* K_1^*, K_2^*, K_3^*)$

Step 4:

  For i=1 to 4

  $ECTC_i(T_4^* \rightarrow T^*) = TC_i(T_4^*, K_i^*) - TC_i(T^*)$

  $SAVING = \sum_{i=1}^{4} ECTC_i$

Step 5:

  For i=1 to 4

$SHARE_i = SAVING * \dfrac{TC_i(T_4^*)}{TC(T_4^*)}$

Figure 7.2: coordination benefits sharing scheme

The first step of the scheme presented in Figure 7.2 computes the basic replenishment cycle favored by the retailers. It also computes their expected total cost per unit time. The second step computes the integer multipliers and corresponding costs for the distributors, the manufacturers and the suppliers in a decentralized fashion. The total costs under the decentralized and centralized policies are computed in the third step. The economic cost consequence of accepting the centralized policy instead of the decentralized policy for each stage is computed in the fourth step. This step also computes the entire supply saving resulting from the coordination. The last step computes the saving share for each stage.

7.9   Numerical Analysis

In this section, we consider an example of a four-stage supply chain having one supplier, three manufacturers, and seven retailers. The relevant data is shown in Table 7.1. The demand at the end retailers is assumed to follow normal distributions. In addition to the data in Table 7.1, it is assumed that the shortage cost per unit time per unit short is 0.08. A local search method can be used to find the optimal solution for this example. Under the equal time mechanism, the optimal cycle time is 0.0447 years and the expected total cost $TC=\$78943.331$ per year. Under the integer multipliers mechanism, the basic cycle time at the retailers is 0.0282 years. The integer multiplier for the suppliers is $K_1=2$, and hence the cycle time at this stage equals 0.1128 years. Also, the integer multiplier for the manufactures and distributors are $K_2=2$ and hence the cycle time at this stage equals 0.0564 years. However $K_3=1$ and consequently the cycle time at this stage is 0.0282 years and the total cost drops by 26.612% ($21008.2004) to $TC=\$57935.127$ per year. Under the powers of two multipliers mechanism, the optimal basic cycle time is 0.007 years and the powers of two $K_1,$ $K2,$ $K3,$ and K_4 are 4, 2,1, and 0 respectively. The expected total cost $TC=\$79004.35$ which higher than the expected total costs under the other two mechanisms.

We perform some sensitivity analysis on saving from using integer multipliers mechanism over the equal time cycle mechanism. We first decrease the current values of the setup cost at the suppliers, distributors, and manufacturers stages by 25%, 50% and finally 75%. The results are given in Table 7.2 and Figure 7.3. From these results it can be concluded that if the setup costs are decreased at the upper stream stages, then the saving from using integer multipliers mechanism over the equal time cycle mechanism will decrease.

We then increase the values of (h_0, h_1, and h_2) by using multipliers of (1.25, 1.50 and 2.00) of the original values. The results presented in Table 7.3 reveal that if the holding costs are increased at the upper stream stages, then the saving from using integer multipliers mechanism over the equal time cycle mechanism will decrease.

Table 7.1: Example data

	j	Set up cost	Holding cost	Demand Mean	variance	Production rate
Retailers	1	100	10	10,000	60	
	2	100	10	20,000	70	
	3	100	10	40,000	85	
	4	100	10	12,000	50	
	5	100	10	24,000	95	
	6	100	10	9,000	75	
	7	100	10	18,000	65	
Distributors	1	200	7	30,000		
	2	200	7	40,000		
	3	200	7	12,000		
	4	200	7	24,000		
	5	200	7	9,000		
	6	200	7	18,000		
Manufacturers	1	600	(0.8,1.5)	70,000		140,000
	2	600	(0.8,1.5)	36,000		108,000
	3	600	(0.8,1.5)	27,000		108,000
Suppliers	1	800	(0.08,0.8)	133,000		399,000

Table 7.2: Sensitivity analysis when (A_1, A_2, A_3) are decreased

(A_1,A_2,A_3) Decrease	25%		50%		75%	
	T*	ETC*	T*	ETC*	T*	ETC*
Equal time cycle	0.0389	69367.796	0.0319	58065.614	0.023	43497.256
Integer multipliers	0.0468	45681.394	0.0386	38663.267	0.028	29658.592
Saving		23,686.4		19,402.35		13,838.66

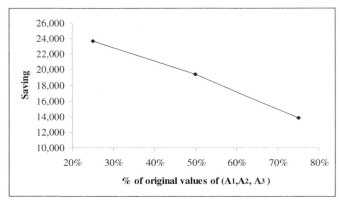

Figure 7.3: Saving in the total cost of integer multipliers over equal cycle

Table 7.3: Sensitivity analysis when (h_0, h_1, and h_2) are increased

(h_0, h_1, and h_2) multipliers	1.25		1.50		2.00	
	T*	ETC*	T*	ETC*	T*	ETC*
Equal time cycle	0.0442	797,994.4546	0.0437	80,636.2371	0.0477	82,292.127
Integer multipliers	0.0515	53613.516	0.0496	55500.851	0.0612	58,840.400
Saving		744,380.9		25,135.39		23,451.73

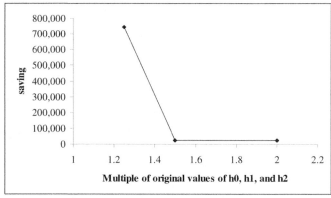

Figure 7.4: Saving in the total cost of integer multipliers over equal cycle

7.10   Summary

In this chapter, we presented a four-stage, non-serial supply chain model is presented. This supply chain system consists of suppliers, manufactures, and retailers. The production rates for the suppliers and manufactures are assumed finite. In addition the demand for each retailer is assumed to be stochastic.

First, the model is formulated under three centralized inventory coordination mechanisms between the chain members. The first mechanism is the equal cycle mechanism. The second mechanism is the integer multiplier mechanism. The third mechanism is the integer powers of two multipliers mechanism. Numerical analysis indicated that integer multiplier mechanism results in lower total cost. The validation of the developed model is given in Appendix B.

Next, the model is formulated under the decentralized policy. This step is needed to develop a scheme that can be used to share the centralized coordination among the supply chain partners.

Chapter 8

Book Contributions and Future Directions

8.1 Introduction

This chapter outlines the main contribution of this research work and the future research directions.

8.2 Contributions

Our contributions are summarized as follows:

(a) A generalized algebraic supply chain optimization model

We reviewed the existing deterministic multi-stage, non-serial supply chain models and developed a generalized algebraic model for optimizing inventory decisions in a multi-stage, complex supply chain. The model is developed under the integer multipliers inventory coordination mechanism.

The developed model extends all the relevant previous work. Some researchers considered this direction as good point for research. For example Cárdenas (2007) considered modeling the integer multipliers coordination for the general multi-stage supply chain as future research. Also Chung (2007) recommended the extension of his work to four stage supply chain as a challenging point of research.

The recursive structures we used to drive the optimal replenishment policy, gave useful insights that helped in developing the proposed solution procedure. It also established the convexity of the cost function with ease. Hence it contributes in the theory and solution methodology. To date, our model could be regarded as a new finding in the area of supply chain modeling. This contribution is available for researchers in Seliaman and Ab Rahman (2008c).

(b) Reconfiguring the network for better coordination

We developed a mathematical model that can be used to support supply chain strategic policy making such as designing the supply chain networks or reconfiguring existing ones. Three different inventory coordination mechanisms were considered while developing the model.

This model extends the model presented in Khouja (2003) to reconfigure the network. Under the new configuration, a firm can supply any customer in the adjacent downstream stage. The researchers may refer to the idea which is presented in Ab Rahman and Seliaman (2007).

(d) Coordination benefits sharing scheme

Fourth, we proposed benefits sharing scheme that will allow all supply chain partners to share the benefits resulting from implementing any of the investigated inventory coordination mechanisms, among the members of the supply chain. Such scheme is essential in order to entice all partners to adopt the centralized coordination mechanisms and motivate their implementation.

The proposed scheme takes into consideration the individual economic cost consequence of accepting any of the centralized coordination by any supply chain partner. Implementing this scheme will result in equal percent saving for all of the supply chain partners. This contribution is available for researchers in Seliaman and Ab Rahman (2008b).

8.3 Future Directions

Obviously, the models presented in this thesis can be enhanced by relaxing more restrictive assumptions. Future research will continue to extend our work in several directions.

Considering variable demand at the end retailers is one direction to extend the deterministic models. While considering the lead time is another direction.

It would very interesting to consider the different inventory coordination mechanism for the multi- product multi-stage supply chain systems. This might also involve questions about scheduling the production for the different products.

It is also possible to extend these models to include quantity discount based coordination mechanisms. Different quantity discount structures can be introduced between the different stages of the supply chain.

Modeling the inventory coordination decisions in a multi-stage supply chain with rework consideration is a possible research opportunity. Developing a model for network configuration under stochastic demand is also possible research direction.

References

1. Ab Rahman, A., and Seliaman, M. E. (2007). Reconfiguring the Supply Chain Network for Better Coordination. In the *Proceedings of the International Conference of Mathematical Sciences*. Bangi-Putrajaya, Malaysia.

2. Al-Fawzan,, M., A.(1997). Mathematical Models for quality in Multi-Stage Production Systems. Ph.D. dissertation. King Fahd University of Peteroleum and Minerals.

3. Al-Sultan, K.S. and Al-Fawzan, M.A. (1997). A tabu search Hooke and Jeeves algorithm for unconstrained optimization. *European Journal of Operational Research*. 103 :198–208.

4. Axsater, S. (2000). *Inventory Control*. Kluwer Academic Publishers Boston/Dordech/ London.

5. Banerjee, A. (1986). A Joint Economic-Lot-Size Model for Purchaser and Vendor. *Decision Sciences*. 17: 292-311.

6. Banerjee, A., Jonathan, B., and Banerjee, S. (2003). Simulation Study of Lateral Shipments in Single Supplier, Multiple Buyers Supply Chain Networks. *International Journal of Production Economics*, Amsterdam: 81/82 : 103.

7. Barnes-Schuster, D., Bassok, Y., and Anupindi, R. (2006). Optimizing Delivery Lead time /Inventory Placement in a Two-Stage Production/Distribution System. *European Journal of Operational Research*. 174:1664-1684.

8. Ben-Daya, M., Darwish, M., and Ertogral, K. (2008). The joint economic lot sizing problem: Review and extensions. *European Journal of Operational Research*. 185 : 726–742.

9. Ben-Daya, M., As'ad, R., and Seliaman, M.,(2010). An integrated production inventory model with raw material replenishment considerations in a three layer supply chain. *International Journal of Production Economics, In Press*, Corrected Proof, Available online 28 October 2010.

10. Ben-daya, M., Al-Nassar, A., (2008). Integrated multi-stage multi-customer supply chain. *Production Planning and Control the Management of Operations*. 19 (2):97–104.

11. Cárdenas-Barrón, L. E (In Press). Optimal manufacturing batch size with rework in a single-stage production system – A simple derivation. *Computers & Industrial Engineering*. doi:10.1016/j.cie.2007.07.017.

12. Cárdenas-Barrón, L. E. (2006). Optimizing Inventory Decisions in a Multistage Multi-Customer Supply Chain: A Note. *Transportation Research Part E: Logistics and Transportation Review*. 43 (5):647–654..

13. Cárdenas-Barrón, L. E. (2007). Optimizing inventory decisions in a multistage multi-customer supply chain: A note. *Transportation Research Part E: Logistics and Transportation Review* .Volume 43, Issue 5, September 2007, Pages 647-654

14. Cárdenas-Barrón, L. E. (2011). The derivation of EOQ/EPQ inventory models with two backorders costs using analytic geometry and algebra. *Applied Mathematical Modelling, Volume 35, Issue 5, May 2011, Pages 2394-2407*

15. Cárdenas-Barrón, L.E., 2001. The economic production quantity (EPQ) with shortage derived algebraically. *International Journal of Production Economics* 70, (3), 289-292.

16. Carter, J., R, Ferrin, B. G, Carter, C. R. (1995). The effect of less-than-truckload rates on the purchase order lot size decision. *Transportation Journal.* Lock Haven. 34(3) pg. 35-45.

17. Chelouah R. and Siarry, P. (2000). Tabu Search applied to global optimization *European Journal of Operational Research.* 123:256-270.

18. Chelouah R. and Siarry, P. (2005). A hybrid method combining continuous tabu search and Nelder–Mead simplex algorithms for the global optimization of multiminima functions. *European Journal of Operational Research.* 161: 636–654.

19. Chen ,J., and Chen, T. (2005). The Multi-Item Replenishment Problem in a Two-Echelon Supply Chain: The Effect of Centralization versus Decentralization. *Computers & Operations Research.* 32: 3191–3207

20. Chen, T., and Chen, J. (2005). Optimizing supply chain collaboration based on joint replenishment and channel coordination. *Transportation Research Part E: Logistics and Transportation Review.* 41(4): 261-285

21. Chiu, S.W. (2008). Production lot size problem with failure in repair and backlogging derived without derivatives. *European Journal of Operational Research.* 188(2),pp 610-615.

22. Chung, C. J. and Wee, H. M. (2007). Optimizing the Economic Lot Size of a Three-Stage Supply Chain with Backordering Derived without Derivatives. *European Journal of Operational Research.* 183:933-943

23. Ding , D. and Chen, J. (2008)Coordinating a three level supply chain with flexible return policies. *Omega.* 36: 865–876.

24. Dumrongsiri , A., Fana, M., Jaina, A. and Moinzadeha, A. (2006). A supply chain model with direct and retail channels. *European Journal of Operational Research.* 187(3): 691-718.

25. El Saadanya, A. M., Jaber, M. Y. (2008). Coordinating a two-level supply chain with production interruptions to restore process quality. *Computers & Industrial Engineering*. 54(1),pp. 95-109.

26. Ellram, L.M. (1991).Supply Chain Management: The Industrial Organization Perspective. *International Journal of Physical Distribution and Logistics Management*. 21(1): 13-22.

27. Ertogral, K., Darwish, M., Ben-Daya, M. (2007). Production and Shipment Lot Sizing in a Vendor-Buyer Supply Chain with Transportation Cost. *European Journal of Operational Research*. 176:1592-1606.

28. Esper, T.,L. and Williams L., R.(2003). The value of Collaborative Transportation Management (CTM): Its relationship to CPFR and information technology. *Transportation Journal*. Lock Haven. 42(4): 55

29. Farahania, R. Z. and Elahipanaha, M. (2008). Genetic algorithm to optimize the total cost and service level for just-in-time distribution in a supply chain. *International Journal of Production Economics*. 111(2),pp. 229-243.

30. Felix T.S. Chan, T. Zhang (2011). The impact of Collaborative Transportation Management on supply chain performance: A simulation approach. *Expert Systems with Applications*, Volume 38, Issue 3, March 2011, Pages 2319-2329.

31. Glover, F. (1989).Tabu search. Part I. *ORSA Journal on Computing* .1 (3): 190-206.

32. Glover, F., and Laguna, M. (1997). Tabu Search. Kluwer Academic Publishers.

33. Goyal, S.K. (1995). A One-Vendor Multi-Buyer Integrated Inventory Model: A Comment. *European Journal of Operational Research*. 82: 209-210.

34. Goyal, S.K. and Gupta Y.P. (1989). Integrated inventory models: The buyer-vendor Coordination. *European Journal of Operational Research*. 41: 261-269.

35. Goyal, S.K. and Nebebe, F. (2000). Determination of Economic Production-Shipment Policy for a Single-Vendor Single-Buyer System. *European Journal of Operational Research*. 121: 175-178.

36. Goyal, S.K. and Szendrovits A.Z.,(1986). A Constant Lot Size Model with Equal and Unequal Sized Batch Shipments between Production Stages. *Engineering Costs and Production Economics*. 10: 203-210.

37. Goyal, S.K., (1976). An Integrated Inventory Model for a Single Supplier-Single Customer Problem. *International Journal of Production Research*.: 107-111

38. Ha, D. and Kim, S. (1997). Implementation of JIT Purchasing: An Integrated Approach. *Production Planning & Control* .8:152-157.

39. Han , C. (2005). Stochastic modeling of a two-echelon multiple sourcing supply chain system with genetic algorithm. *Journal of Manufacturing Technology Management*. 16(1): 87-108.

40. Hedar, A. and Fukushima, M. (2006). Tabu Search directed by direct search methods for nonlinear global optimization. *European Journal of Operational Research*. 170: 329–349.

41. Hill, R.M. (1997). The-single vendor single-buyer integrated production-inventory model with a generalized policy. *European Journal of Operational Research*.7: 493-499.

42. Hill, R.M. (1999). The optimal production and shipment policy for the single-vendor single-buyer integrated production-inventory problem. *International Journal of Production Research*. 37: 2463-2475

43. Hooke, R. and Jeeves, T. A. (1961). Direct Search Solution of Numerical and Statistical Problems. *Journal of the Association for Computing Machinery*. 212-229.

44. Hoque, M. A. (2008). Synchronization in the single-manufacturer multi-buyer integrated inventory supply chain. *European Journal of Operational Research*. 188: 811–825.

45. Houqe, M.A. and Goyal, S.K. (2000). An optimal policy for a single-vendor single-buyer integrated production-inventory system with capacity constraint of the transport equipment. *International; Journal of Production Economics* 65. pp 305-315.

46. Hua, Z. and Li, S. (2008). Impacts of demand uncertainty on retailer's dominance and manufacturer-retailer supply chain cooperation. *Omega* 36 : 697–714.

47. Hwarang, H., Chong, C, Xie, N. and Burgess, T.(2005). Modeling Compless supply chain: Understanding the Effect of Simplified assumptions. *International Journal of Production research*. 43(13) 2829-2872

48. Jaber, M. and Rosen, M. A. (2007). The economic order quantity repair and waste disposal mode. *European Journal of Operational Research*.188(1), pp. 109-120.

49. Kang, J., and Kim, Y,.(2010). Coordination of inventory and transportation managements in a two-level supply chain. International Journal of Production Economics, Volume 123, Issue 1, January 2010, Pages 137-145.

50. Karabatı, S., and Sayına, S. (2008). Single-supplier/multiple-buyer supply chain coordination: Incorporating buyers' expectations under vertical information sharing. *European Journal of Operational Research*. 187(3)pp. 746-764.

51. Khouja, M. and Goyal, S.(2008). A review of the joint replenishment problem literature: 1989-2005. *European Journal of Operational Research*. 186:1-16

52. Khouja., M. (2003) Optimizing Inventory Decisions in a Multi-Stage Multi-Customer Supply Chain. *Transportation Research. Part E, Logistics & Transportation Review*. Exeter. 193-208.

53. Kim, S., W. and Park, S. (2008). Development of a Three-Echelon SC Model to Optimize Coordination Costs. *European Journal of Operational Research*.184:1044-1061.

54. Kit-Nam Francis Leung (2008).Using the complete squares method to analyze a lot size model when the quantity backordered and the quantity received are both uncertain. *European Journal of Operational Research*. 187(1)pp:

55. Lee ,H.L., Padmanabhan, V. Whang, S. (1997). The Bullwhip Effect in Supply Chains. *Sloan Management Review*. 93-102.

56. Lee, H. T., Wu, J.C.(2006) A study on inventory replenishment policies in a two-echelon supply chain system. *Computers & Industrial Engineering* 51 : 257–263.

57. Lee, Young Hae , Cho, Min Kwan; Kim, Yun Bae. (2002). A Discrete-Continuous Combined Modeling Approach for Supply Chain Simulation. *Simulation*. 78(5): 321-329.

58. Leung, Kit-Nam Francis (2010). A generalized algebraic model for optimizing inventory decisions in a centralized or decentralized multi-stage multi-firm supply chain. *Transportation Research Part E: Logistics and Transportation Review*, Volume 46, Issue 6, November 2010, Pages 896-912.

59. Li, J., and Liu, L. (2006). Supply chain coordination with quantity discount policy. *Int. J. Production Economics*.101:89–98.

60. Long, Z., Shiji , S., and Cheng , W. (2005). Supply Chain Coordination of Loss-Averse Newsvendor with Contract. *Tsinghua Science &Technology*. 10(2): 133-140.

61. Lu, L.(1995). A One-Vendor Multi-buyer Integrated Inventory Model. *European Journal of Operational Research*. 81: 312-323.

62. Man-Yi, T., and Xiao-Wo, T. (2006). The Further Study of Safety Stock under Uncertain Environment . *Fuzzy Optimization and Decision Making.* 5(2): 193-202.

63. Nagarajan, M. and Sošić, G. (2008).Game-theoretic analysis of cooperation among supply chain agents: Review and extensions. *European Journal of Operational Research.* 187(3), pp. 719-745.

64. Nahmias, S. (2001). *Production and Operations Analysis.* Fourth Edition McGraw-Hill/Irwin

65. Ouenniche, J. and Boctor, F. F. (2001). The multi-product, economic lot-sizingproblem in flow shops:the powers-of-two heuristic. *Computers & Operations Research.* 28:1165-1182.

66. Pujaria, N. A., Trevor, S. and Faizul Huq. (2008). A continuous approximation procedure for determining inventory distribution schemas within supply chains. *European Journal of Operational Research.* 186(1),pp. 405-422 .

67. Rajesh., P., Viswanathan., S.(2003). A Model for Evaluating Supplier-Owned Inventory Strategy. *International Journal of Production Economics,* Amsterdam. 81/82: 565

68. Rau, H. and OuYang, B. C. (2008).An optimal batch size for integrated production–inventory policy in a supply chain. *European Journal of Operational Research.* 185(2),pp 619-634.

69. Ross, D.(1998). Competing Through Supply Chain Management: Creating Market-Winning Strategies Through Supply Chain Partnerships. New York: Chapman & Hill.

70. Santos, T., Ahmed, S., Goetschalckx, M., and Shsairo, A. (2005) . A Stochastic Programming Approach for Supply Chain Network Design under Uncertainty. *European Journal of Operational Research.* 167:96-115.

71. Sarmah, S.P., Acharya, D., and Goyal, S.K.(2006). Buyer vendor coordination models in supply chain management. *European Journal of Operational Research*.175: 1–15.

72. Scott, J. M., P Mauricio, R., Jennifer, A. F, and Randall, G. K. (2003). Integrating the Warehousing and Transportation Functions of the Supply Chain. *Transportation Research. Part E, Logistics & Transportation Review,* Exeter. 39(2): 141.

73. Seliaman, M. E., and Ab Rahman, A. (2008a). Optimizing inventory decisions in a multi-stage supply chain under stochastic demands. *Applied Mathematics and Computation* Elsevier Inc. 206(2): pp.538-542

74. Seliaman, M. E., and Ab Rahman, A. (2008c) A Generalized Algebraic Model for Optimizing Inventory Decisions in a Multi-Stage Complex Supply Chain.. *Transportation Research Part E*. Elsevier Inc. 45:pp.409-418.

75. Seliaman, M. E., and Ab Rahman, A.(2008b). Proposed Scheme for Sharing the Benefits of the Supply Chain Coordination. *In the Proceedings of ICMSAO' 09* , JANUARY 20-22 2009 , SHARJAH,

76. Seliaman, M. E., and Ab Rahman,(2007). Simulation Analysis of a Perishable Supply Chain. In the proceedings of *The Fourth Saudi Technical Conference and Exhibition*, 02-06 December 2006, Riyadh, Kingdom of Saudi Arabia.

77. Seliaman, M. E., and Ab Rahman,(2010). Modeling the Coordinated Supply Chain Network. *Journal of Quality Measurement and Analysis (JQMA)*, 6(2), pp. 87-94.

78. Shapiro, J. F. (2001). *Modeling the Supply Chain*. First Edition, DUXBURY, Thomson Learning.

79. Simch-Levi, D. Kaminsky, P. and Simch-Levi, E (2003) *Designing &Managing the Supply Chain: Concepts , Strategies, and Case Studies*. Second Edition, McGraw-Hill.

80. Smitha, S., Petty, D., Trustrum, D., Labib, A. and Khan, A.(2008). A supply network-modeling system for a small- to medium-sized manufacturing company. *Robotics and Computer-Integrated Manufacturing*. In Press. Corrected Proof.

81. Steven, G.C. (1989). Integrating the Supply Chain. *International Journal of Physical Distribution and Logistics Management*. 8(8): 3-8.

82. Tee, Y. and Rossetti,M. (2002). A Robustness Study of a Multi-echelon Inventory Model vi Simulation. *International Journal of Production Economics*. 80: 265-277

83. Tempelmeier, H. (2006). On the Stochastic Uncapacitated Dynamic Single-Item Lotsizing Problem with Service Level Constraints. *European Journal of Operational Research*.

84. Tsiakis, P., and Papageorgiou, L. G. (2008). Optimal production allocation and distribution supply chain networks. *International Journal of Production Economics*. 111(2) 468-483.

85. Viswanathan, S.(1998). Optimal Strategy for the Integrated Vendor-Buyer Inventory Model. *European Journal of Operational Research*. 105: 38-42.

86. Waller, M., Johnson, M. ., Davis, T. (1999). Vendor-managed inventory in the retail supply chain. *Journal of Business Logistics*. Oak Brook: 20(1) 183-2 04.

87. Wee, H. M., and Chung, C. J. (2007). Note on the economic lot size of the integrated vendor–buyer inventory system derived without derivatives. *European Journal of Operational Research*.177 (2), pp: 1289-1293.

88. Weng, Z. K., and McClurg, T. (2003). Coordinating Ordering Decisions for Short Life cycle Products with Uncertain in Delivery Time and Demand. *European Journal of Operational Research*. 151:12-24.

89. Yao , M., and Chiou, C. (2004). On a replenishment coordination model in an integrated supply chain with one vendor and multiple buyers. *European Journal of Operational Research*. 159(2): 406-419.

90. Yao, M. and Elmaghraby, S. E.(2001). The Economic Lot Scheduling Problem under Power-Of-Two Policy. *Computers and Mathematics with Applications*. 41: 1379-1393.

Appendices

Appendix A

Explanation of how we derived the structures in section 3

From Eq. (5.24) the total cost for the entire supply chain is

$$TC = T \left\{ \frac{ADh_n + \sum_{i=1}^{n-1}\sum_{j} IC_{i,j}A}{2A} \right\} + \frac{1}{T}\sum_{i=1}^{n} \frac{S_i}{\prod_{s=i}^{n} K_s} \qquad (A.1)$$

Substituting $IC_{i,j} = \dfrac{\prod_{s=i}^{n} K_s TD_{i,j}^2 h_{i-1}}{2P_{i,j}} + \dfrac{\prod_{s=i+1}^{n} K_s TD_{i,j}}{2}(K_i(1+D_{i,j}/P_{i,j})-1)h_i$ in

Eq.(A.1) we get:

$$TC = T \left\{ \frac{ADh_n + \sum_{i=1}^{n-1}\sum_{j}\left(\dfrac{\prod_{s=i}^{n} K_s TD_{i,j}^2 h_{i-1}}{2P_{i,j}} + \dfrac{\prod_{s=i+1}^{n} K_s TD_{i,j}}{2}(K_i(1+D_{i,j}/P_{i,j})-1)h_i \right)A}{2A} \right.$$

$$\left. + \frac{1}{T}\sum_{i=1}^{n} \frac{S_i}{\prod_{s=i}^{n} K_s} \right\} =$$

$$T/2A\left\{ADh_n + \sum_{i=1}^{n-1}\sum_j\left(\prod_{s=i}^n K_s TD_{i,j}^2 h_{i-1}\bigg/2P_{i,j} + \prod_{s=i+1}^n K_s TD_{i,j}\bigg/2(K_i(1+D_{i,j}/P_{i,j})-1)h_i\right)A\right\}$$

$$+\frac{1}{T}\sum_{i=1}^n\frac{S_i}{\prod\limits_{s=i}^n K_s}$$

$$=$$

$$\frac{T}{2A}\left\{\begin{array}{l}ADh_n + \\ K_{n-1}(h_{n-2}+h_{n-1})\sum_j D_{n-1,j}^2 B_{n-1,j} + K_{n-1}Ah_{n-1}\sum_j D_{n-1,j} - Ah_{n-1}\sum_j D_{n-1,j} + \\ K_{n-1}K_{n-2}(h_{n-3}+h_{n-2})\sum_j D_{n-2,j}^2 B_{n-2,j} + K_{n-1}K_{n-2}Ah_{n-2}\sum_j D_{n-2,j} - K_{n-1}Ah_{n-2}\sum_j D_{n-2,j} + \\ \cdots\cdots\cdots\cdots\cdots\cdots\cdots\cdots\cdots\cdots\cdots\cdots\cdots\cdots\cdots\cdots\cdots\cdots\cdots\cdots\cdots\cdots\cdots + \\ \cdots\cdots\cdots\cdots\cdots\cdots\cdots\cdots\cdots\cdots\cdots\cdots\cdots\cdots\cdots\cdots\cdots\cdots\cdots\cdots\cdots\cdots\cdots + \\ \prod_{s=2}^n K_s(h_1+h_2)\sum_j D_{2,j}^2 B_{2,j} + \prod_{s=2}^n K_s Ah_2\sum_j D_{2,j} - \prod_{s=3}^n K_s Ah_2\sum_j D_{2,j} + \\ \prod_{s=1}^n K_s(h_0+h_1)\sum_j D_{1,j}^2 B_{1,j} + \prod_{s=1}^n K_s Ah_1\sum_j D_{1,j} - \prod_{s=2}^n K_s Ah_1\sum_j D_{1,j}\end{array}\right\}$$

$$+\frac{1}{T}\sum_{i=1}^n\frac{S_i}{\prod\limits_{s=i}^n K_s}\tag{A.2}$$

where B_{ij} is product of all production rates at stage i except firm j.
Rearranging the terms of Eq. (A.2) we get:

$$\frac{T}{2A}\left\{\begin{array}{l}ADh_n - Ah_{n-1}\sum_j D_{n-1,j} + \\ K_{n-1}\left[\begin{array}{l}(h_{n-2}+h_{n-1})\sum_j D_{n-1,j}^2 B_{n-1,j} + K_{n-1}Ah_{n-1}\sum_j D_{n-1,j} - Ah_{n-2}\sum_j D_{n-2,j} + \\ K_{n-2}\left[\begin{array}{l}(h_{n-3}+h_{n-2})\sum_j D_{n-2,j}^2 B_{n-2,j} + Ah_{n-2}\sum_j D_{n-2,j} - Ah_{n-3}\sum_j D_{n-3,j} + \\ \cdots\cdots \\ K_2\left[\begin{array}{l}(h_1+h_2)\sum_j D_{2,j}^2 B_{2,j} + Ah_2\sum_j D_{2,j} - Ah_1\sum_j D_{1,j} + \\ K_1\left[(h_0+h_1)\sum_j D_{1,j}^2 B_{1,j} + Ah_1\sum_j D_{1j}\right]\end{array}\right]\cdots\cdots\end{array}\right]\end{array}\right\}$$

$$+\frac{1}{T}\sum_{i=1}^n\frac{S_i}{\prod\limits_{s=i}^n K_s}\tag{A.3}$$

Now substituting the recursive structures of Eq.(5.25),Eq.(5.26), and Eq. (5.27) into Eq.(A.3), we get:

$$TC = \frac{T}{2A}\left\{\begin{matrix} ADh_n - Ah_{n-1}\sum_j D_{n-1,j} + \\ K_{n-1}\left[\begin{matrix}\alpha_{n-1}+ \\ K_{n-2}\left[\begin{matrix}\alpha_{n-2} \\ \cdots\cdots \\ K_2\left[\begin{matrix}\alpha_1+ \\ K_1[\psi_0+\alpha_0]\end{matrix}\right]\cdots\cdots\end{matrix}\right]\end{matrix}\right]\end{matrix}\right\}$$

$$+\frac{1}{T}\left(S_n+\frac{\varphi_{n-1}}{K_{n-1}}\right)$$

$$=\frac{T}{2A}\left(K_{n-1}\psi_{n-1}+\alpha_{n-1}\right)+\frac{1}{T}\left(S_n+\frac{\varphi_{n-1}}{K_{n-1}}\right) \tag{A.4}$$

Substituting Eq.(5.29) and Eq.(5.30) into Eq.(A.4) we get:

$$TC = TY + \frac{W}{T} \tag{A.5}$$

Appendix B

Validation of the Stochastic Model

The objective of this section is to verify and validate the stochastic model developed in chapter 7. We first show that the expected cycle inventory levels at the distributors, manufacturers, and suppliers described for the deterministic demand can be used even under the stochastic demand. Second simulation is used to validate our optimization search procedure.

Verifying the Development of the Analytical Model

Shin and Benton (2007) showed that for a two-stage supply chain structure, the supplier's expected cycle inventory level under the uncertain demand is the same as the one under deterministic demand. Lemma B.1 below extends the arguments of Shin and Benton (2007) to the case of four-stage supply chain.

Lemma B.1: The deterministic inventory level at each of the distributors, manufacturers and suppliers can be used to approximate the inventory levels at these stages for stochastic environment.

Proof: In chapter 5, we developed the expected holding inventory per unit time at an end retailer as given by (7.1). We first show that under stochastic demand the average inventory level at distributors converges to $(K_3 - 1)Q/2$ if the end retailers order a fixed quantity Q in the four-stage continuous review supply chain system. Assume that the retailers orders arrive at random times: $\tau_0, \tau_1, \tau_2, ..., \tau_i$. As in Shin and Benton (2007) we show that the expected moment for each of the retailers' orders arrival times under stochastic demand $(E[\tau_i])$ is the same as the retailers' orders arrivals under deterministic demand $(E[T_i])$.

Let $\lfloor(Q-m_Q)/D\rfloor$ be the absolute deviation of the deterministic order arrival moment T_i from the realized location of τ_i.

Now the location of T_i can be represented in terms of the relative deviation from the actual τ_i, as:

$$T_i = E[\tau_i + (Q - m_Q)/\bar{a}] = E[\tau_i] + E[(Q - m_Q)/\bar{a}]$$
$$= E[\tau_i] + (1/\bar{a})E[Q - m_Q]$$

Where $\bar{a}$ is the expected demand during the ordering cycle.

$$E[Q - m_Q] = \int_{-\infty}^{\infty} (Q - m_Q) f(m_Q) d(m_Q) = 0$$

This means that:

$$E[\tau_i] = T_i$$

Hence, the average inventory level at the distributors' stage can be determined as

$$(K_3 - 1)Q/2$$

Now, similar arguments can be used to show that the average inventory level at the manufacturers converges to $\dfrac{K_3 Q}{2}(K_2(1 + D_2/P_2) - 1)$ if the distributors order a fixed quantity $K_3 Q$. These steps can also be applied to show that the average inventory level at the suppliers converges to $\dfrac{K_2 K_3 Q}{2}(K_1(1 + D_1/P_1) - 1)$ if the manufacturers order a fixed quantity $K_3 K_3 Q$. This completes the proof that the deterministic inventory level at each of the distributors, manufacturers and suppliers can be used to approximate the inventory levels at these stages for stochastic environment. The details of driving the expected inventory level under stochastic demand are presented in section 7.3. In our model the stochastic nature of the demand is forced at the retailers' stage. In the next section we use using discrete event simulation to evaluate our analytical model and the optimization algorithm.

Validating the Model Using Simulation

To operationally validate our analytical model, a simulation model was developed to represent the four stage supply chain system described in chapter 5. The simulation is built in ProModel 7.0. Our developed analytical model is based on the assumption of continuous time domain for the demand at the end retailers. However, it is difficult to reflect the continuous nature of the demand process when using discrete event simulation modeling (Lee and Cho, 2002). To overcome this problem, the basic cycle time at the retailers' level is divided to approximate the continuous demand pattern. We obtained the optimal values $(T_1^*, K_1^*, K_2^*, K_3^*)$ from our analytical model, and these values are used in the simulation model. In the simulation model we followed fixed-increment time approach. The time increment used is λ which equals one tenth of the retailers' basic cycle time T^* as calculated by our optimization algorithm. The cycle time at the distributors' stage is $K_3^* T^*$. The cycle time at the manufacturers is $K_2^* K_3^* T^*$. The cycle time at the suppliers is $K_1^* K_2^* K_3^* T^*$. Because the demand function depends on the length of the cycle time T^*, in the simulation model we approximate the demand distribution function as follows:

$f_4(x, T)$ With the following parameters:

$\mu = \lambda.D$

$\sigma = \lambda.\sigma$

This approximated function is reached by experiments and is different than the closed form function used in the analytical model.

The developed simulation model has been verified and validated using two approaches. In the first approach deterministic input values are used for the demand to run the simulation. The systems states are checked and found to agree logically with the constant input values. In the second approach the animation of the inventory system is observed. This animation reflected a reasonable performance of the simulation model. Figure B.1 shows the inventory level at the retailers stage under deterministic demand while Figure B.2 shows the inventory level at the retailers stage under stochastic demand.

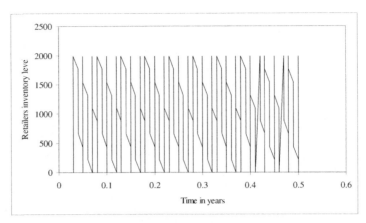

Figure B.1: Retailers inventory level for deterministic demand

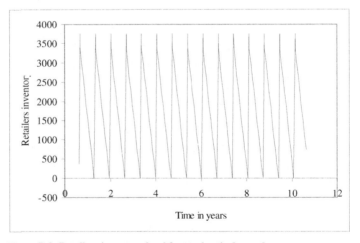

Figure B.2: Retailers inventory level for stochastic demand

In our simulation analysis we considered the supply chain system as a non-terminating system. We used the average inventory level at the end retailers as our performance measure. Ten replications were used to run the simulation model. Each replication is of run length 2.8 years. To evaluate the performance of the developed analytical model, the deviation of the model value from the simulated value is used for comparison. The relative error is defined as:

Error =Analytical Model Value- Simulation Model Value

Relative Error= Error/ Simulation Model Value

We used our optimization procedure to solve the for stage supply chain system with data presented in Table 7.1 of chapter 7. The solution obtained by the optimization procedure is used to test the model. The recommended inventory replenishment policy is used to run the simulation. The results of the simulation analysis are summarized in Table B.1.

Table B.1: Retailers average inventory: the error and relative error

Replication	Simulated Value	Model value	Error	Relative error
1	1707.925	1302.123	405.80	0.2379
2	1708.665	1302.123	406.54	0.2375
3	1707.603	1302.123	405.48	0.2374
4	1707.569	1302.123	405.45	0.2379
5	1708.643	1302.123	406.52	0.2373
6	1707.198	1302.123	405.08	0.2369
7	1706.363	1302.123	404.24	0.2373
8	1707.178	1302.123	405.05	0.2381
9	1709.011	1302.123	406.89	0.2363
10	1704.932	1302.123	402.81	0.2363
Average	1707.509	1302.123	405.39	0.2374

The simulation results show that the analytical model tends to underestimate the average inventory level at the end retailers with a deviation of about 24% of the simulated value. The underestimation of the average holding inventory is possibly due to the modeling of the continuous demand distribution as discrete. Another perspective to explain this deviation is that the use of close-form time dependent demand distribution. Similar results are reported in the literature even for supply chain models with more simplified assumptions and less number of stages. For example, Hwarng et al. (2005) reported a deviation of 70% in the average inventory holding when modeling a supply chain system under simplified demand and lead time assumptions. Tee and Rossetti (2002) used simulation to evaluate the robustness of two-echelon inventory model. Their simulation results reported a cost relative error that ranged between 21% and 40%.

Printed in Great Britain
by Amazon

84101332R00071